FUNDAMENTALS OF TOTAL QUALITY & BUSINESS ERGONOMICS

The Art of Quality and Job Role Management

Ms. Jyothi NT
Dr. P. Ebby Darney

Fundamentals Of Total Quality & Business Ergonomics

Copyright © 2025 Dr. P. Ebby Darney And Ms. Jyothi NT

All rights reserved. No part of this book may be reproduced, stored in a retrieval system, or transmitted in any form or by any means, electronic, mechanical, photocopying, recording, or otherwise, without the prior written permission of the author.

This book is sold as is, without any warranties, express or implied. The author and publisher are not responsible for any problems that may arise from using this book. If you have a problem with the book, your only option is to return it for a refund. The author agrees to protect the publisher from any legal issues that may arise from the book's content. Any legal disputes about this book will be handled according to the laws of the constitution of India

Publisher: Inkscribe Publishing Pvt. Ltd.

ISBN Number: 978-1-966421-92-4

Quality check by discovering the bad ones and throwing them out is too late & vain, Excellence comes not from inspection but from improvement of the methods

— **Ms. Jyothi NT**

Ergonomics is the discipline of fixing the job to an employee and an invention to its user. Manage the cause, not the result

— **Dr. P. Ebby Darney**

Module I - INTRODUCTION TO TQM

Defining Quality, Basic approaches of TQM, Gurus of TQM - Shewart, Ronald Fisher, Deming, Juran, Feigenbaum, Ishikawa, Crosby, Taguchi – TQM Framework – Historical review, Obstacles, Benefits of TQM

Module II: TQM PRINCIPLES

Leadership, Customer Satisfaction, Employee Involvement, Continuous Process Improvement, Supplier Partnership, Performance Measures, Cost of Quality.

Module III: TOOLS AND TECHNIQUES –1

Benchmarking, Information Technology, ISO 9000 Series of Quality Management Systems - Environmental Management Systems.

Module IV: TOOLS AND TECHNIQUES- 2

QFD, FMEA, Quality Circles, TPM, Traditional Quality Tools and Management tools.

Module V: IMPLEMENTATION OF TQM

Steps in TQM implementation, national and international quality awards, case studies.

Module VI INTRODUCTION MANEGEMENT ERGONOMICS

The themes of Ergonomics – scarcity and efficiency – three fundamental economic problems – society's capability – Production possibility frontiers (PPF) – Productive efficiency Vs economic efficiency – economic growth & stability – Micro economies and Macro economies – the role of markets and government – Positive Vs negative externalities.

Module VII CONSUMER AND PRODUCER BEHAVIOUR

Market – Demand and Supply – Determinants – Market equilibrium – elasticity of demand and supply – consumer behaviour – consumer equilibrium – Approaches to consumer behaviour – Production – Short-run and long-run Production Function – Returns to scale – economies Vs diseconomies of scale – Analysis of cost – Short-run and long-run cost function – Relation between Production and cost function.

Module VIII PRODUCT AND FACTOR MARKET

Product market – perfect and imperfect market – different market structures – Firm's equilibrium and supply – Market efficiency – Economic costs of imperfect competition – factor market – Land, Labour and capital – Demand and supply – determination of factor price – Interaction of product and factor market – General equilibrium and efficiency of competitive markets.

Module IX PERFORMANCE OF AN ECONOMY – MACRO ECONOMICS

Macro-economic aggregates – circular flow of macroeconomic activity – National income determination – Aggregate demand and supply – Macroeconomic equilibrium – Components of aggregate demand and national income – multiplier effect – Demand side management – Fiscal policy in theory.

Module X: AGGREGATE SUPPLY AND THE ROLE OF MONEY

Short-run and Long-run supply curve – Unemployment and its impact – Okun's law – Inflation and the impact – reasons for inflation – Demand Vs Supply factors –Inflation Vs Un employement tradeoff – Phillips curve – short- run and long-run –Supply side Policy and management- Money market- Demand and supply of money – money-market equilibrium and national income – the role of monetary policy

AUTHOR PROFILE:

Ms. JYOTHI NT

A visionary woman leader dedicated herself to shaping individuals with strong ethical values and a deep sense of social responsibility. As the President of LIPS Research Foundation, she plays a pivotal role in fostering Research, education, and skill development to empower individuals of our nation for a better future.

In her role as the Chief Director of LIPS Gurukulam, A training division under Ministry of Information & Broadcasting, she is committed to equipping individuals, regardless of their background field, with essential skills and training to enhance their employability and contribute to a developed nation. LIPS Gurukulam is designed to sharpen knowledge and provide specialized learning opportunities tailored to industrial interests, societal needs, and establish a government of India-driven Skill and certified program.

Additionally, as the Director of DL CARD registered under MSME since 1976, Jyothi NT is instrumental in shaping young minds through International & industry Certified junior level Courses, catering to children aged 6 to 18, ensuring a solid foundation for their careers and a progressive society. A passionate supporter for women's empowerment, she prioritizes creating educational and job opportunities for women, offering them the necessary support and encouragement to succeed. Her unwavering commitment to inclusivity and skill development continues to drive meaningful change in society.

Dr. P EBBY DARNEY

The Vice President of LIPS Research, the advanced research and development wing of the European International University, Paris, France. In this capacity, he plays a pivotal role in steering innovative academic and applied research initiatives across interdisciplinary domains.

Dr. Darney is also a visionary mentor and educator, actively involved in LIPS Gurukulam, a transformative platform dedicated to nurturing young, aspiring minds through holistic and research-driven learning methodologies. With a strong inclination towards innovation and applied science, Dr. Darney holds 11 patents, spanning both design and utility categories. His inventive contributions reflect a consistent pursuit of real-world problem solving and product development. An accomplished academic, Dr. Darney has authored and published over 65 research articles in peer-reviewed and reputed international journals, contributing significantly to the body of knowledge in engineering, technology, and interdisciplinary studies. In addition to his academic and research roles, he is an Advisory Member of Aerozjet Pvt. Ltd., where he offers strategic insights into technological advancement in the aerospace sector. He is also a life member of the Indian Society for Technical Education (ISTE), demonstrating his long-standing commitment to the advancement of technical education in India and beyond. Dr. Ebby Darney's professional journey is characterized by his dedication to innovation, education, and mentorship, making him a respected figure in both academic and industrial landscapes.

DEDICATION

I dedicate this book to my LIPS team and learners, who inspired in me the true value of purpose; to my exceptional educators, who helped turn vision into action; and to every aspiring leader and management thinker — may this book fuel your journey toward innovation, impact, and excellence.

— **Ms. Jyothi NT**

I wholeheartedly dedicate this book to my fellow faculty members, whose values and unwavering support have shaped my journey; to my incredible team, whose dedication and belief transformed vision into reality; and to all those passionate about management studies — may this work inspire you to lead with purpose, think strategically, and grow with confidence.

— **Dr. P. Ebby Darney**

ACKNOWLEDGMENTS

First of all, my parents, who always stood by my side, encouraged me and blessed me with love. The man who groomed my efforts is none other than Dr. Lal. I feel highly privileged to express my sincere regards and gratitude to him for his dynamic leadership, expert supervision, and valuable suggestions. He not only motivated me but also guided me with his skilled knowledge whenever I approached him. The present accomplishment would not have seen the light of day if I had not received the unstinted cooperation of my LIPS Team

— **Ms. Jyothi NT**

I would like to express my special appreciation and thanks to our LIPS advisor, Dr. Lal. You have been a tremendous motivation for me. I would like to thank my friends & team for encouraging me to explore and for forcing me to implement. That advice for my career has been priceless.

Words cannot express how grateful I am to my mother, father, and family for all of the sacrifices that you've made on my behalf. Your prayer for me was what sustained me thus far-

— **Dr. P. Ebby Darney**

MODULE I

INTRODUCTION TO TQM

Defining Quality, Basic approaches of TQM, Gurus of TQM - Shewart, Ronald Fisher, Deming, Juran, Feigenbaum, Ishikawa, Crosby, Taguchi – TQM Framework – Historical review, Obstacles, Benefits of TQM

Total Quality Management is a continuous process of detecting and eliminating manufacturing errors, streamlining supply chains, improving the customer experience, and ensuring employees are fully trained.

UNDERSTANDING TOTAL QUALITY MANAGEMENT (TQM):

Total quality management is a structured approach to overall organizational management. The focus of the process is to improve the quality of an organization's outputs, including goods and services, through the continual improvement of internal practices. The standards set as part of the TQM approach can reflect both internal priorities and any industry standards currently in place.

Industry standards can be defined at multiple levels and may include adherence to various laws and regulations governing the operation of a particular business. Industry standards can also include the production of items to an understood norm, even if the norm is not backed by official regulations.

PRIMARY PRINCIPLES OR BASIC APPROACHES OF TQM:

1. Focus on Customers: Customer input is highly valued because it allows a company to better understand the needs and requirements in the manufacturing process. Customer surveys may reveal insufficient durability of goods.
2. Commitment by Employees: This includes clearly communicating across departments and leaders what goals, expectations, needs, and constraints are in place. A company adopting TQM principles must be willing to train employees and give them sufficient resources to complete tasks successfully and on time.
3. Improve Continuously: A company should gradually evolve and strive for incremental, small improvements as it learns more about its customers, processes, and competition. This concept of continuous improvement helps a company adapt to changing market expectations.
4. Adherence to Processes: Every member engaged in the process must be aware and educated on their part of the process to ensure proper steps are taken at the right time of production. These processes are then continually analyzed to better understand deficiencies in the process.
5. Strategic and Systematic Approach: A company's processes and procedures should be a direct reflection of the organization's vision, mission, and long-term plan. TQM calls for a system approach to decision-making that requires that a company dedicate itself to integrating quality as its core component and making the appropriate financial investments to make that happen.

6. Overall Data Utilization: Management must continually rely on production, turnover, efficiency, and employee metrics to correlate the anticipated outcomes with the actual results.
7. Integrate Systems: One way to utilize data is to integrate systems. TQM strategies believe systems should talk to each other, conveying useful information across departments and making smart decisions.
8. Communication: Effective communication plays a large part in TQM to motivate employees, educate members along a process, and avoid process errors, whether it is normal day-to-day operations or large organizational changes.
9. Supplier Partnership: Suppliers play a critical role in delivering quality. Building strong relationships ensures better inputs and mutual success. Collaborate with suppliers, set clear expectations, and establish quality standards for procurement.
10. Holistic Culture : Quality is embedded in the organizational culture, ensuring every individual values and contributes to it. Promote leadership commitment, recognize achievements, and maintain open communication about quality initiatives.

Hence, in the context of Total Quality Management (TQM), quality can be defined as:

"MEETING OR EXCEEDING CUSTOMER EXPECTATIONS CONSISTENTLY BY DELIVERING PRODUCTS, SERVICES, OR PROCESSES THAT ARE FREE OF DEFECTS AND ALIGNED WITH THE DESIRED SPECIFICATIONS."

Also, Total Quality Management consists of three qualities that are as follows:-

1. Quality of return to satisfy the needs of shareholders.
2. Quality of products and services to satisfy some specific needs of the consumers.
3. Quality of life at work and outside work to satisfy the needs of the people in the organization.

Gurus of TQM:

1. WALTER A SHEWHART

One of the most notable contributors to modern industry is Walter Shewhart, a quality control pioneer. He started his rise to guru status as a Bell Telephone employee in 1918. Born in New Canton, Illinois in 1891, Shewhart set precedents that would be referenced for years to come in establishing the importance of information distribution among quality managers and production personnel.

Walter Shewhart is known today as the "father of statistical quality control," or simply, SQC. Modern generation managers adopted his philosophy as the "Six Sigma" approach for quality assurance. Walter Shewhart died on March 11th, 1967 in Troy Hills, New Jersey; a genius, an innovator, a visionary, and a legend in his not only own time, but for decades thereafter. His Key Ideas were, [ ] Shewhart Charts: Common vs Special Causes:

While at Bell Labs, Shewhart revolutionized their production process. This ensured greater economic gains in the form of reducing the need for repair of the equipment the labs produced. He referenced what constituted "common causes" and "special causes" of production issues. He analyse these with his famed Shewhart charts or control charts, Walter Shewhart laid the statistical foundation upon which all modern industry would be built.

"Common causes" in quality assessment is best represented by imagining one cursive printing the word "cat," five times; it's natural to expect some minor variation from word to word, but in general each attempt would appear relatively the same. Minor variations such as these are considered "common causes" in the world of quality control.

If, on the other hand, during the writing process the writer is bumped and writes a skewed letter, this variation in word is considered a "special cause" in the world of quality control. It's the goal of Shewhart's control charts to identify and track these types of variations with the intent to both monitor and identify possible patterns. This info supplies quality control managers with the tools necessary to minimize and eliminate "special causes," which affects the company's bottom line.

PDSA Cycle or Shewhart Cycle:

Walter Shewhart also created the Shewhart Cycle or PDSA (plan, do, study, act) cycle, the scientific method for learning through action as well as observation.

To illustrate: if a company isn't experiencing the success it would like in each area, the company is wise to brainstorm ideas for improvement. This is the "plan" phase of the cycle.

Next, the company chooses a course of action to pursue, then pursues it, which logically, constitutes the "do" phase.

The "study" phase that follows consists of the company observing the results of their actions, and subsequently, making judgments as to their efficacy. This step is crucial. It serves as the foundation for the next and final "act" phase.

The "act" phase instructs the company to analyze the observed results. If the results are pleasing, change course to pursue this direction further. If they are not, this phase instructs the company to circle back to the original brainstorming pool in order to start the process over again and repeat the cycle until the company is pleased with the results.

This plan illustrates Shewhart's ideas that continual evaluation of management procedures and management's consideration of new ideas are vital in streamlining "common causes" and mitigating "special causes" in variation.

2 RONALD FISHER

- Ronald Fisher was a pioneering British statistician and geneticist who made significant contributions to the development of modern statistical methods, particularly in the areas of experimental design, analysis of variance, and the foundations of statistical inference. His work had a profound impact on various fields, including biology, agriculture, and social sciences. Fisher's ideas and techniques are deeply rooted in the topics of One-Way ANOVA, the F Distribution, and the F Ratio.
- Analysis of Variance (ANOVA): A statistical method developed by Fisher to compare the means of two or more groups by analysing the variance within and between the groups.
- F Distribution: A probability distribution used in hypothesis testing, particularly in the context of ANOVA, to determine the significance of the differences between group means.
- F Ratio: A test statistic calculated in ANOVA that compares the variance between groups to the variance within groups, used to determine if the differences between group means are statistically significant.

- The One-Way ANOVA lab lets students apply Ronald Fisher's statistical methods, including ANOVA, the F distribution, and the F ratio, to analyse real-world data. By testing hypotheses, analysing variance, and interpreting statistical significance, students gain practical insight into Fisher's groundbreaking contributions and their lasting impact on modern statistics.

- One of the most famous approaches to experimental design developed by Fisher is randomization, a method for randomly assigning treatments or interventions to experimental groups to avoid bias. Fisher also introduced the technique of randomized blocks to control external variables that might affect the results of the experiment, increasing experimental efficiency by reducing unwanted variability.

- Fisher was also renowned for his work in statistical estimation theory, particularly in developing Maximum Likelihood Estimation (MLE). MLE is a method for estimating the parameters of a distribution based on observed data. This method works by choosing the parameter values that maximize the likelihood of the observed data under a given probabilistic model. MLE has become a very important technique in statistics and is widely used in various applications, ranging from regression analysis to more complex probabilistic modeling.

3. W. EDWARDS DEMING

- Deming's Theory Also called Deming's Theory of Profound Knowledge, Deming's Theory is a management philosophy based on systems theory. Deming's Theory is a system-based management philosophy framework that "represents a holistic approach to leadership and management."

- Appreciation for a sytem: Leaders must understand and optimize all parts of a system collectively, rather than focusing on individual components.
- Knowledge of Variation: Issues often arise from system flaws, not individuals.

Identifying and addressing variations in workflows or processes leads to improvement.

- Theory of Knowledge: Continuous learning, questioning, and improvement are essential. Deming's PDSA (Plan-Do-Study-Act) cycle enables small-scale, low-risk testing and refinement of changes before broader implementation. He popularised PDSA Cycle.
- Knowledge of Psychology: Understanding human behaviour helps leaders motivate and manage teams effectively, optimizing the overall system.
- Deming developed a set of 14 key principles for management transformation, which he believed were essential for achieving quality excellence. Some of these points included creating constancy of purpose, adopting a new philosophy of cooperation, and driving out fear from the workplace.

EDWARDS DEMING'S 14 POINTS:

I. Create constancy of purpose for improving products and services.

II. Adopt the new philosophy.

III. Cease dependence on inspection to achieve quality.

IV. End the practice of awarding business on price alone; instead, minimize total cost by working with a single supplier.

V.	Improve constantly and forever every process for planning, production and service.
VI.	Institute training on the job.
VII.	Adopt and institute leadership.
VIII.	Drive out fear.
IX.	Break down barriers between staff areas.
X.	Eliminate slogans, exhortations, and targets for the workforce.
XI.	Eliminate numerical quotas for the workforce and numerical goals for management.
XII.	Remove barriers that rob people of pride of workmanship and eliminate the annual rating or merit system.
XIII.	Institute a vigorous program of education and self-improvement for everyone.
XIV.	Put everybody in the company to work accomplishing the transformation.

4 JOSEPH M. JURAN

- Dr. Joseph M. Juran is considered by many to be the father of many of the quality management techniques still used in industry today. Dr. Juran's quality management approach is based on three key principles. The first is application of the Pareto principle – also known as the "80/20 rule." In the context of quality, this means identifying "the vital few and the trivial many" – in other words, the small percentage of root causes in manufacturing or service processes that account for the largest effect in terms of defects or cost.

- The second principle of Juran's approach to quality is management theory. This involves a change of thinking away from mere focus on the quality of the end product, to a wider examination of the human dimension of quality management. Education and training for managers in the workplace is as important as the nuts and bolts of the manufacturing process, while other human factors such as resistance to change also need to be accounted for. Juran's management theory was fundamental in expanding quality management principles beyond the factory floor to principles that could also be applied to service-related processes.

- The final principle consists of three processes often known collectively as the **Juran Trilogy**. These three elements are quality planning (the design stage), quality control (ongoing inspections to ensure that processes are in control) and quality improvement (including proactive refinement of processes to improve processes).

The Components of Juran's Quality Trilogy

Quality Planning:

The first phase of the trilogy, quality planning, sets the foundation for meeting customer expectations. It involves defining who the customers are, determining their needs, and developing product features that respond to those needs. The key activities in this phase include:

- Establish Quality Goals: Determine what customers need and define these needs as quality goals.

- Identify the Customers: Recognize both internal and external customers. Understanding who will be impacted by the products or services is crucial.
- Determine Customer Needs: Engage with customers to accurately capture all their requirements and expectations to adequately plan to meet them.
- Develop Product Features: Translate customer needs into actionable product features that meet these needs.
- Develop Process Features: Establish processes capable of producing these features consistently while meeting the goals set.
- Establish Process Controls: Implement and maintain controls that ensure the process performs as planned.

Quality Control:

The second component, Quality Control, focuses on executing the plans created during the Quality Planning phase. It involves monitoring operations to detect deviations from set standards and to signal when action is necessary. Essential activities include:

- Evaluate Actual Performance: Measure existing operations to assess whether they meet the quality goals established in the planning phase.
- Compare Actual Performance to Quality Goals: Regularly compare results to quality goals to identify gaps.
- Act on the Difference: When performance deviates from quality standards, corrective action must be taken to align outcomes with goals.

Quality Improvement:

The final phase of the trilogy is Quality Improvement. This phase is about creating measures to improve existing conditions continuously. Unlike Quality Control, which focuses on maintaining current success, Quality Improvement aims at elevating the standard. Key activities involve:

- Prove the Need for Improvement: Establish clear evidence that processes are not performing adequately or could perform better.

- Identify Improvement Projects: Pinpoint specific areas where improvements can be made.

- Organize for Improvement: Create teams and assign responsibilities to carry out improvement projects.

- Diagnose the Causes: Determine the root causes of deficiencies to address them effectively.

- Provide Remedies and Establish Controls: Implement solutions to rectify the root causes and put controls in place to sustain improvements.

5. ARMAND V FEIGENBAUM

- Armand V. Feigenbaum is a towering figure in the field of quality management. His groundbreaking work laid the foundation for what would become a global movement in improving organizational quality. Feigenbaum's contributions are significant, particularly his introduction of Total Quality Control (TQC), which later evolved into the widely adopted concept of Total Quality Management (TQM).

- Feigenbaum introduced the concept of Total Quality Control in his seminal book, "Total Quality Control," published in 1951. At the heart of TQC is the idea that quality is not the responsibility of a single department but a collective responsibility that permeates every level of an organization. Feigenbaum's TQC philosophy includes several key principles:

i. **Comprehensive Quality Focus:**

Feigenbaum argued that quality should not be confined to the production floor but should encompass every aspect of the organization, from design and engineering to marketing and customer service. This holistic approach ensures that quality is built into the product from the very beginning. By involving all departments in quality initiatives, organizations can identify and address potential issues early in the process, leading to better products and services.

ii. **Quality Control as a System:**

He emphasized that quality control should be a systemic effort, integrating all organizational functions and processes. This integration ensures that every department works towards common quality goals, creating a cohesive and efficient system. By viewing quality control as an interconnected system, organizations can streamline their operations and eliminate redundancies, resulting in improved overall performance.

iii. **Cost of Quality:**

Feigenbaum introduced the concept of the cost of quality, which includes prevention costs, appraisal costs, and failure costs. He argued that investing in quality control measures early on can significantly reduce the costs associated with defects and failures in the long run. By understanding and managing these costs, organizations can make informed decisions about where to allocate resources for the greatest impact on quality and profitability.

iv. **Continuous Improvement:**

One of the key elements of TQC is the idea of continuous improvement. Feigenbaum believed that organizations should always strive to enhance their processes, products, and services through incremental improvements and innovations. This commitment to continuous improvement ensures that organizations remain competitive and can adapt to changing market conditions and customer expectations.

Armand V. Feigenbaum is also known for his concept of the "hidden plant". That is – in every factory a certain proportion of its capacity is wasted through not getting it right the first time. Dr. Feigenbaum quoted a figure of up to 40% of the capacity of the plant being wasted. At that time, this was an unbelievable figure; even today some managers are still to learn that this is a figure not too far removed from the truth.

6 KAORU ISHIKAWA

- Kaoru Ishikawa is considered the 'Father of Japanese Quality' for his creation of innovative developments in quality management. He is famous for creating the fishbone diagram, a type of 'root cause analysis' which we still use in Quality Improvement (QI) to help make decisions and create actions. Ishikawa is a hugely respected figure in Quality Improvement, having been instrumental in developing quality initiatives in Japan.

- When the industrial sector changed after the Second World War in Japan, Kaoru Ishikawa met Deming and Juran. They worked together to develop management concepts that are still in use.

Ishikawa invented the concept of 'quality circles' in 1960. Quality circles are groups of people who meet to improve organisational performance. Although the only company to take part in the original 'quality circles' study was Nippon Telephone and Telegraph, the study was a great success and went on to gain traction and become more and more popular as part of the concept of Total Quality management (TQM).

Ishikawa also created the concept of 'Internal Customers' highlighting how important employees are to any organisation.

- Ishikawa had a huge input into the development of Total Quality Management and to Process improvement Methodologies. He had a strong belief that you should service your customers even after they have bought your organisation's products. Ishikawa was also instrumental in creating processes to address customers' needs which led to better quality and process efficiency. He came up with the policy of "the next process is your customer," which encourages better cooperation within a company. Ishikawa also promoted the fact that high level personnel should be able to always support their teams and was a firm believer that they should take quality control courses.

- Fishbone Diagram (Cause & Effect Diagram)
  The Fishbone diagram - also known as the Ishikawa diagram and the cause and effect diagram - was developed and created by Ishikawa and was originally used to analyse the cause of problems within quality management. It's called Fishbone Diagram due its shape – the head stating the 'problem', and the bones showing the various causes.

It is known as one of the seven quality control tools.

The tool can help you identify major causes and indicate the most fruitful areas for further investigation. It will help you understand the problem more clearly. By going through the process of building the diagram with colleagues, everybody gains insights into the problem, alongside possible solutions. Ishikawa also showed the importance of the seven quality tools: control chart, run chart, histogram, scatter diagram, Pareto chart, and flowchart.

Fig: Basic Quality Tools

7. PHILIP B. CROSBY

- Philip B. Crosby, a renowned figure in the field of quality management, revolutionized the way organizations approach quality. With his groundbreaking concepts of "Zero Defects" and "Quality is Free," Crosby has left an indelible mark on modern quality practices.

- The concept of **"Zero Defects"** is arguably Crosby's most renowned contribution. Introduced in the 1960s while he was working at the Martin Company, Crosby's philosophy was simple yet profound: defects are not acceptable and should be prevented, not inspected out. This marked a significant departure from the prevailing notion that defects were inevitable and acceptable within certain limits. Crosby believed that quality could be achieved through a mindset shift, where every employee was responsible for ensuring their work was free of defects. He argued that defects were not a result of employee incompetence but rather of poorly designed processes and systems.

- Implementation: Crosby implemented the Zero Defects program at the Martin Company, focusing on building quality into processes from the start. His approach emphasized the importance of doing things right the first time, reducing the need for rework and inspection. This proactive strategy involved extensive training and fostering a culture of accountability among employees.

Crosby's implementation included clear communication of quality standards, rigorous training programs, and an emphasis on employee empowerment. By involving every level of the organization in the quality process, Crosby ensured that the Zero Defects philosophy was not just a top-down mandate but a collective goal.

- Another groundbreaking concept introduced by Crosby is "Quality is Free." In his 1979 book of the same name, Crosby argued that investing in quality improvement efforts is cost-effective because the cost of poor quality—defects, rework, customer dissatisfaction—far exceeds the cost of prevention.

Crosby's assertion was that quality should not be viewed as an expense but as a means to reduce overall costs. By preventing defects and focusing on quality from the outset, organizations could save money that would otherwise be spent on rework, repairs, and dealing with customer complaints.

Crosby's Four Absolutes of Quality Management,

i. Definition of Quality: Crosby defined quality as conformance to requirements, emphasizing that quality should be measured by whether products and services meet specified standards. This clear definition helped organizations establish measurable quality goals and track their performance effectively.

ii. The System of Quality: According to Crosby, quality is achieved through prevention, not inspection. He argued that quality should be built into processes from the beginning, rather than relying on end-of-line inspections to catch defects. This proactive approach reduces defects and associated costs.

iii. Performance Standard: Crosby introduced the performance standard of "Zero Defects," challenging the notion that defects are inevitable. He advocated for a mindset of doing things right the first time, setting a high bar for quality performance.

iv. Measurement of Quality: Crosby proposed measuring quality by the cost of non-conformance, i.e., the cost of doing things wrong. By quantifying the financial impact of poor quality, organizations could make informed decisions about investing in quality improvement initiatives.

8 GENICHI TAGUCHI

- Genichi Taguchi was a Japanese engineer and statistician who significantly impacted the field of quality control and improvement. His pioneering work in the development of robust design techniques, known as Taguchi Methods, has been instrumental in advancing product quality and performance. This article delves into his contributions and key concepts, focusing on Taguchi Methods and the Loss Function.

- Taguchi's method emphasizes using **Design of Experiments (DoE)** to efficiently improve product quality by investigating multiple variables simultaneously. It simplifies traditional DoE through orthogonal arrays, which reduce the number of experimental runs while studying multiple factors. Additionally, Taguchi introduced signal-to-noise (S/N) ratios to assess product or process robustness by comparing the desired outcome to background noise, making it highly effective for industrial applications.

- Robust design is the cornerstone of Taguchi Methods. It involves designing products and processes to be inherently stable and consistent, regardless of external noise factors. Taguchi categorized factors into three types:

    - Control Factors: Variables that can be controlled and set during the design process.
    - Noise Factors: Variables that are difficult or expensive to control and can cause variability in performance.
    - Signal Factors: Variables that directly affect the output or response of the system.

- By focusing on control factors and making the product or process robust against noise factors, Taguchi's methods aim to ensure consistent performance under a wide range of conditions.

    In practical terms, robust design involves identifying and optimizing control factors to minimize the effect of noise factors on the product's performance. This approach results in products that perform consistently and reliably, even in the presence of variations in manufacturing conditions, environmental factors, or usage scenarios.

- Taguchi's Loss Function quantifies the economic loss due to deviations from target performance, emphasizing customer satisfaction and cost impact over traditional defect-based quality measures. It is mathematically expressed as: The Loss Function is mathematically expressed as:

    $L(y) = k(y - T)^2$

Where, **L(y)** is the loss, **y** is the actual value, **T** is the target, and **k** scales the loss.

- This quadratic relationship emphasizes that even small deviations from the target can lead to significant economic loss. The Loss Function shifts the focus from merely meeting specifications to achieving optimal performance, thereby enhancing overall quality and customer satisfaction. Significance is that this highlights the cost of variability, stressing that even small deviations can lead to significant economic losses, shifting the focus to achieving optimal performance.

- Applications:

    - Identify critical quality characteristics. o Set target values based on customer needs.

    - Reduce variability using robust design methods.

FRAMEWORK OF TQM

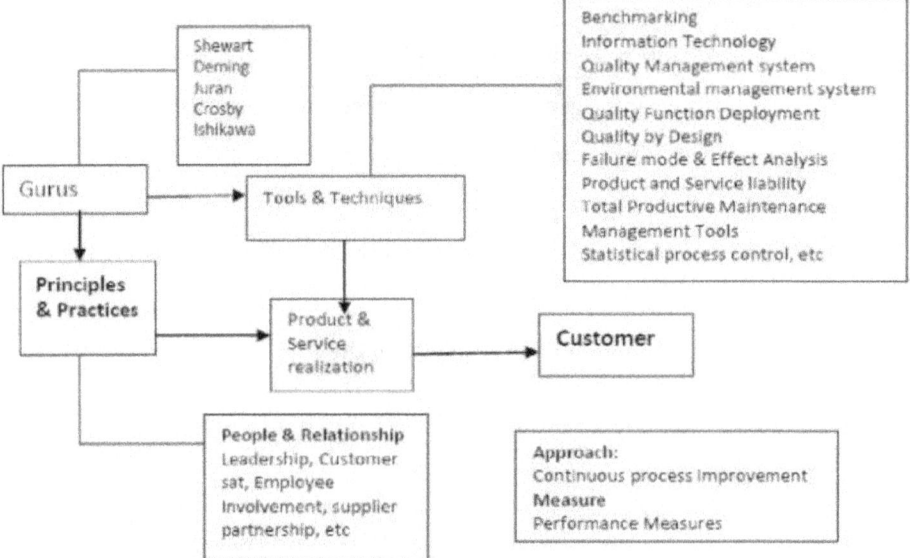

Fig: Graphical Representation of TQM Framework

The Total Quality Management (TQM) Framework focuses on achieving long-term success by enhancing customer satisfaction and organizational performance. It emphasizes continuous improvement, teamwork, and customer-centered practices. Here's an outline of the framework:

Key Components of the TQM Framework:

    i.   Customer Focus:

        •Understand and meet customer needs and expectations.

        •Treat customer satisfaction as the goal of quality efforts.

  .ii   Leadership

- Leaders set a vision and direction for quality initiatives.
- Foster a culture of commitment to quality and continuous improvement.

iii. Employee Involvement

- Engage employees at all levels in quality processes.
- Provide training and encourage teamwork to promote collaboration.

iv. Process Approach

- Manage activities and resources as processes to improve efficiency.
- Focus on optimizing workflows for better outcomes.

v. Continuous Improvement

- Commit to ongoing efforts to improve products, services, and processes. Utilize methods like Plan-Do-Check-Act (PDCA) for iterative progress.

vi. Fact-Based Decision Making

- Use data and analysis to guide decisions| | Rely on evidence rather than assumptions for problem-solving.

vii. Integrated System

- Align processes, departments, and teams toward achieving organizational goals.
- Ensure quality management is integrated into all aspects of the business.

viii. Mutually Beneficial Supplier Relationships

- Develop partnerships with suppliers to enhance value.
- Ensure suppliers adhere to quality standards.

HISTORICAL REVIEW OF THE TQM FRAMEWORK

The development of Total Quality Management (TQM) is rooted in the evolution of quality concepts and practices. Here's a historical timeline that highlights key milestones in its formation:

Early 20th Century: Foundations of Quality Control

1900s: Frederick Taylor introduced Scientific Management, focusing on standardization and efficiency in manufacturing.

- 1920s: Walter A. Shewhart developed the concept of Statistical Process Control (SPC) and introduced the Control Chart at Bell Telephone Labs. This was a major step toward quality measurement.

- 1930s: Ronald Fisher pioneered the Design of Experiments (DoE), contributing to robust methodologies for process improvement.

1940S–1950S: BIRTH OF QUALITY MANAGEMENT

- 1940s (World War II): Quality became critical for wartime production. The U.S.

  military used Shewhart's methods to ensure quality in defense manufacturing.

- 1950s: W. Edwards Deming and Joseph Juran brought quality management principles to Japan, focusing on system thinking and continuous improvement. Deming introduced his 14 Points for Management and the PDSA cycle. Juran emphasized the Quality Trilogy: planning, control, and improvement.

1960S–1970S: EVOLUTION OF TQM CONCEPTS

- 1960s: Armand Feigenbaum introduced the term Total Quality Control, emphasizing organization-wide quality practices. Kaoru Ishikawa developed the Fishbone Diagram (Cause-and-Effect Diagram) to identify root causes of quality issues. Philip Crosby promoted Zero Defects and the concept that quality is free when done right the first time.

- 1970s: Quality circles became popular in Japan as a means of engaging employees in problem-solving. The concept of Robust Design by Genichi Taguchi introduced the Loss Function to quantify the economic impact of variability.

1980S: TQM GAINS GLOBAL RECOGNITION

1980s: TQM was formalized as a comprehensive management philosophy, integrating principles of leadership, employee involvement, and process improvement. Companies like Toyota led the way with Lean Manufacturing and the Toyota Production System (TPS). Malcolm Baldrige National Quality Award (U.S.) and Deming Prize (Japan) incentivized organizations to adopt TQM.

1990S–2000S: INTEGRATION WITH MODERN PRACTICES

- 1990s: TQM merged with ISO 9000 standards, offering a structured approach to quality assurance. Six Sigma emerged as a complementary methodology focusing on defect reduction and process improvement.

- 2000s: Organizations began integrating TQM with Lean principles and Agile methodologies for greater flexibility and efficiency. **Present Day: Continuous Evolution**

- Modern TQM incorporates digital tools like AI and IoT to enhance data collection and analysis for process optimization. Emphasis on sustainability and corporate social responsibility (CSR) has expanded the scope of quality beyond products to include environmental and social impacts.

OBSTACLES OF TQM

- Lack of Management Commitment.

- Inability to change Organizational Culture.

- Improper Planning.

- Incompatible organizational structure and Isolated individual departments.

- Lack of Continuous Training and Education.

- Ineffective Measurement Techniques, lack of access to data

- Inadequate use of Empowerment and Teamwork
- Failure to Improve Continually

MODULE II

TQM PRINCIPLES

Leadership, Customer Satisfaction, Employee Involvement, Continuous Process Improvement, Supplier Partnership, Performance Measures, Cost of Quality.

A commonly known quality management approach is Total Quality Management (TQM). This philosophical approach focuses on leading and achieving quality excellence in every aspect of an organization. It emphasizes continuous improvement, involving all employees in the pursuit of customer satisfaction.

TQM fosters a culture where quality is ingrained, encouraging teamwork, proactive problemsolving, and a commitment to excellence. By integrating quality into all processes and departments, TQM aims to eliminate defects, streamline operations, reduce waste, and enhance overall performance, ensuring long-term success and competitiveness in the market.

The key principles of TQM include:

- Leadership
- Customer Satisfaction
- Employee Involvement
- Continuous Process Improvement
- Supplier Partnership
- Performance Measures
- Cost of Quality

Let's go to the detailed description of the above,

1. Leadership: The process of influencing others towards the accomplishment of goals. He triggers the will to do, shows the direction and guide the group members towards the accomplishment.

CHARACTERISTICS OF QUALITY LEADERS

- Customers first
- Value people
- Build suppler partnership.
- Empower people.
- Strive for excellence.
- Demonstrate involvement / commitment.
- Explain & deploy policy.
- Improve communication.
- Promote teamwork.
- Benchmark continuously.
- Establish system.
- Encourage collaboration.

Strong leadership sets the direction for quality initiatives and ensures that they are aligned with the overall goals of the company. Here's why leadership is key to TQM: • Vision and Commitment: Leaders must establish a clear, shared vision of quality that aligns with the organization's mission and values. They must be committed to promoting quality improvement at every level of the organization.

- Creating a Quality Culture: Leadership is responsible for embedding a quality-first mindset throughout the organization. This involves encouraging behaviors, values, and practices that prioritize quality in all aspects of work.

- Empowerment: Effective leaders empower employees to take ownership of quality improvement. By involving all staff in decision-making and problem-solving, leaders enable everyone to contribute to achieving high-quality outcomes.

- Resource Allocation: Leaders are responsible for providing the necessary resources— such as time, training, and tools—that allow employees to implement quality improvements effectively.

- Leading by Example: Leadership must model quality practices. When leaders demonstrate commitment to quality, it inspires others to follow suit and reinforces the importance of quality within the organization.

- Continuous Learning: Leaders encourage and support learning and development within the organization, ensuring that employees have the skills and knowledge necessary to improve processes and contribute to quality initiatives.

2. Customer Satisfaction: The Customer is the King - Emphasized by Today's Buyers' Market. TQM's Purpose is meeting or exceeding customer expectations, so that the customers are delighted. The customer satisfactions must be the primary goal of any organization. Understanding and meeting customer needs is the priority.

Customers, the most important people in the business

- Not dependent on the organization, but the organization depends on them.
- Not an interruption to work but are the purpose of it.
- Doing a favour when they seek business and not vice-versa.
- A part of business, not outsiders and they are life blood of the business

- People who come with their needs and jobs • Deserve the most courteous and attentive treatment.

SIGNIFICANCE OF CUSTOMER RETENTION

- 60% of organizations future revenue will come from existing customers.

- 2% increase in customer retention has 10% decreases in operating cost.

- 96% of unhappy customers do not complain but 3 times likely to convey to other customers about their bad experience.

- 91% of unhappy customers never purchase goods and services from you.

- It costs 5 times more to attract the customer than retaining the existing customer.

- Customer retention creates customer loyalty and moves customer satisfaction to a next level called customer delight.

SOLVE CUSTOMER COMPLAINTS

- Complaints can be collected from all sources (letters, phone-calls, meetings and verb inputs)

- Develop procedures for complaint resolution, that include empowering frontline personnel.

- Analyse complaints but understand that complaints do not always fit into new categories. Work to identify process and material variations and then eliminate the root cause.

- When a survey response is received, a senior manager should contact the customer and strive to resolve the concern.

- Establish customer satisfaction measures and constantly monitor them.
- Communicate complaint information, as well as the result of all investigation solution, to all people in the organization..
- Provide a monthly complaint report to the quality council for their evaluation and needed, the assignment of process improvement teams.
- Identify customer's expectations beforehand rather than afterward through complaint analysis.

3. Employee Involvement: Encourage and empower employees at all levels to contribute ideas and efforts in a continuous effort to achieve quality improvement.

Total employee involvement integrates quality throughout the production cycle. Quality-related issues and other immediate process issues are addressed promptly.

It is the total involvement from every person at all levels in the organization.

ASPECTS OF EMPLOYEE INVOLVEMENT

i.   Employee motivation
ii. Employee Empowerment
iii. Teams and Teamwork
iv. Recognition and Reward Schemes
v.   Performance Appraisal

EMPLOYEE MOTIVATION: It is the process of stimulating people or attempting to influence other to do your will or accomplish desire goals through the possibility of reward.

- Improves employee involvement.
- Reduces absenteeism and increases turn over.
- Promotes job satisfaction.

EMPLOYEE EMPOWERMENT: It is an environment in which people have the ability, the confidence and the commitment to take his responsibility and ownership to improve the process and initiate the necessary steps to satisfy customer requirements within well-defined boundaries to achieve organizational values and goals.

Job Enrichment: Is expanding content of the Job. Job Empowerment: Is expanding the context of the job.

GENERAL PRINCIPLES OR CHARACTERISTICS FOR EMPOWERING EMPLOYEES

- •Tell people what their responsibilities are.
- •Given the authority equal to the responsibility assigned to them.
- •Set standards of excellence.
- •Give them knowledge information and feedback.
- •Trust them and treat them with dignity and respect.

TEAMS AND TEAMWORK: A team can be defined as a group of people working together to achieve common objectives or goals. Teamwork is the cumulative actions of the team during which each member of the team subordinates his individual interest and opinions for the fulfilling of objectives of the group.

STAGES OF TEAM DEVELOPMENT

- Forming stage- Initial stage with only group of individuals and no teamwork. Team purpose, roles are created.

- Storming Stage - Initial agreement roles are challenged. Hostilities, emerge which may be resolved.
- Norming Stage - Formal informal relations get established.
- Performing Stage - Team operates in a successful manner with trust, openness, healthy conflict, and decisiveness among the members.
- Maintenance stage – Functioning should not deteriorate with time.
- Evaluating Stage – Evaluating team performance.

RECOGNITION AND REWARD SCHEMES: Recognition is a process whereby management shows acknowledgement (Verbal or written) of an employee outstanding performance. Recognition is a form of employee positive motivation. Reward is a tangible one such as increased salaries, commission, cash bonus, gain sharing etc., to promote desirable behaviour. It can be even theatre tickets, dinner for two, a small cash awards, etc., The employees are recognized to improve their morale, show the company's appreciation for Better Performance, create satisfied and motivated workplace, and stimulate creative efforts.

PERFORMANCE APPRAISALS: It is a systematic and objective assessment or evaluation of performance and contribution of individual Needs Identifying employees for salary revision, promotion, transfer, demotion, lay off to determine training needs of employee, to take organizational inventory of people, to know personal strength and weakness of individuals, to validate the selection procedure.

BENEFITS OF PERFORMANCE APPRAISAL

- Provides feedback to identify employees for salary revision, transfer, lay-off
- Helps in determining training needs of employee.
- Provides organization inventory of people.

- Helps to evaluate personal strength and weakness of individuals.

4. Continuous Process Improvement: The core component of TQM is the commitment to delivering quality and the continuous effort to improve the quality of products and services. TQM strives to achieve excellence and total quality control as part of the strategic plan of optimizing and improving processes.

Continuous improvement Significance:

- Ongoing Adaptation: Markets, technologies, and customer preferences are constantly changing. Continuous improvement ensures organizations can adapt effectively and stay ahead of the curve.

- Incremental Progress: Rather than waiting for major changes, continuous improvement emphasizes small, consistent enhancements that accumulate over time to produce significant results.

- Prevention Over Correction: By continuously evaluating and refining processes, potential problems can be identified and resolved before they escalate, reducing waste and inefficiencies.

- Engaged Workforce: Continuous improvement fosters a culture where every employee is encouraged to contribute ideas for betterment, promoting teamwork and innovation.

- Customer-Centric Approach: With a focus on consistently improving quality and efficiency, organizations can better meet customer needs, enhancing satisfaction and loyalty.

- **Efficiency and Cost Savings:** Small, regular improvements help eliminate redundancies, streamline workflows, and optimize resource utilization, ultimately reducing costs.

- **Sustainability and Growth:** Continuous improvement lays the foundation for long-term success by building resilience and fostering a culture of excellence.

By embedding continuous improvement into its operations, an organization not only maintains relevance but also achieves a competitive edge, ensuring it evolves and thrives in a dynamic environment.

5. Supplier Partnership: Supply chain management is a critical component of modern quality control. Companies collaborate closely with suppliers to ensure joint quality planning, from basic raw materials and inputs, as part of an integrated system of business processes and production processes.

PRINCIPLES OF CUSTOMER / SUPPLIER RELATION

- Both the customer and the supplier are fully responsible for the control quality.

- Both the customer and the supplier should be independent of each other and respect each other's independence.

- The customer is responsible for providing the supplier with clear and sufficient requirements so that the supplier can know precisely what to produce.

- Both the customer and the supplier should enter a non-adversarial contract with respect to quality, quality, price, delivery method and terms of payments.

- The supplier is responsible for providing the quality that will satisfy the customer and submitting necessary data upon the customer's request.

- Both the customer and the supplier should decide the methods to evaluate the quality of the product or service to the satisfaction of both parties.

- Both the customer and the supplier should establish in the contract the method by which they can reach an amicable settlement of any disputes that may arise.

- Both the customer and the supplier should continually exchange information, sometimes using multifunctional teams, to improve the product or service quality. • Both the customer and the supplier should perform business activities such as procurement, production and inventory planning, clerical work, and system so that an amicable and satisfactory relationship is maintained.

- When dealing with business transactions both the customer and the supplier should always have the best interest of the end user in mind.

BENEFITS OF SUPPLIER PARTNERING

- Improved Quality
- Reduced cost • Increased Productivity
- Increased efficiency
- Increased market share
- Increased opportunity for innovation
- Continuous improvement of products/services.

A long-term partnership creates opportunities for growth for both parties. As the organization grows, suppliers benefit from increased business, and as suppliers innovate, the organization gains access to better products and services.

By investing in supplier partnerships, organizations can build a robust, efficient supply chain that supports their quality objectives and long-term success.

6. Performance Measures: Performance measurement in TQM serves as a compass that guides organizations towards continuous improvement. It enables companies to evaluate their processes, identify bottlenecks, and make informed decisions based on data-driven insights. Without a robust performance measurement system, organizations may struggle to identify areas of improvement and may miss out on opportunities to enhance customer satisfaction and overall quality. By implementing performance measurement in TQM, companies can foster a culture of accountability and ensure that quality remains a top priority throughout the organization.

Key Metrics for performance Measurement in TQM:

When it comes to measuring performance in TQM, organizations need to identify and track relevant metrics that align with their quality goals. Some key metrics commonly used in TQM include:

Defect Rate: This metric measures the number of defects or errors identified in a process or product. By monitoring the defect rate, organizations can identify areas for improvement and take corrective actions to reduce defects, thereby enhancing quality.

Cycle time: Cycle time refers to the total time required to complete a process or deliver a product or service. By measuring cycle time, organizations can identify bottlenecks and streamline their processes to improve efficiency and meet customer expectations.

Customer satisfaction: Measuring customer satisfaction is crucial in TQM, as it provides insights into how well an organization is meeting customer needs and expectations. Surveys, feedback forms, and Net Promoter Score (NPS) are some common methods used to gauge customer satisfaction.

Employee Engagement: Engaged employees are more likely to contribute to quality improvement initiatives. Organizations can measure employee engagement through surveys or by tracking turnover rates, absenteeism, and employee satisfaction scores.

Cost of Quality: This metric measures the total cost incurred by an organization to prevent, detect, and fix defects. By tracking the cost of quality, organizations can identify areas of waste and allocate resources more effectively.

Role of Performance Measurement in TQM Success:

- Defining Quality Standards: Sets benchmarks for quality and success.

- Monitoring Progress: Tracks improvement initiatives and identifies trends.

- Facilitating Continuous Improvement: Pinpoints inefficiencies and enables refinements.

- Driving Accountability: Assigns measurable goals and fosters ownership.

- Enhancing Decision-Making: Provides data-driven insights for informed strategies.

- Customer Focus: Aligns metrics with customer satisfaction and expectations.

- Encouraging Employee Involvement: Motivates contributions and recognizes achievements.

- Alignment with Strategic Goals: Ensures efforts align with organizational objectives.

- Competitive Advantage: Enhances adaptability, efficiency, and market leadership.

7. Cost of Quality: Cost of quality (COQ) is defined as a methodology that allows an organization to determine the extent to which its resources are used for activities that prevent poor quality, that appraise the quality of the organization's products or services, and that result from internal and external failures. Having such information allows an organization to determine the potential savings to be gained by implementing process improvements.

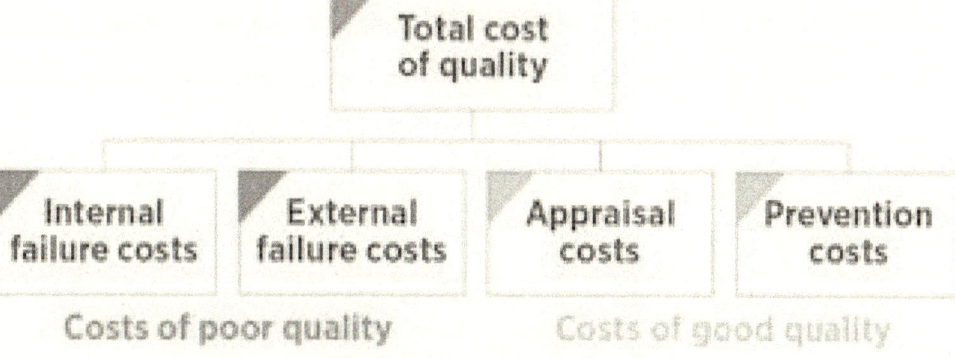

Fig: Breakup of Cost of quality

Appraisal costs:

Appraisal costs are associated with measuring and monitoring activities related to quality. These costs are associated with the suppliers' and customers' evaluation of purchased materials, processes, products, and services to ensure that they conform to specifications. They could include:

- Verification: Checking of incoming material, process setup, and products against agreed specifications.

- Quality audits: Confirmation that the quality system is functioning correctly.

- Supplier rating: Assessment and approval of suppliers of products and services.

Internal failure costs:

Internal failure costs are incurred to remedy defects discovered before the product or service is delivered to the customer. These costs occur when the results of work fail to reach design quality standards and are detected before they are transferred to the customer. They could include:

- Waste: Performance of unnecessary work or holding of stock because of errors, poor organization, or communication.
- Scrap: Defective product or material that cannot be repaired, used, or sold • Rework or rectification: Correction of defective material or errors.
- Failure analysis: Activity required to establish the causes of internal product or service failure.

External failure costs:

External failure costs are incurred to remedy defects discovered by customers. These costs occur when products or services that fail to reach design quality standards are not detected until after transfer to the customer. They could include:

- Repairs and servicing: Of both returned products and those in the field
- Warranty claims: Failed products that are replaced or services that are reperformed under a guarantee.
- Complaints: All work and costs associated with handling and servicing customers' complaints.

- Returns: Handling and investigation of rejected or recalled products, including transport costs.

Prevention Costs:

Prevention costs are incurred to prevent or avoid quality problems. These costs are associated with the design, implementation, and maintenance of the quality management system. They are planned and incurred before actual operation, and they could include:

- Product or service requirements: Establishment of specifications for incoming materials, processes, finished products, and services.
- Quality planning: Creation of plans for quality, reliability, operations, production, and inspection.
- Quality assurance: Creation and maintenance of the quality system.
- Training: Development, preparation, and maintenance of programs.

Cost of quality and organizational objectives

The costs of doing a quality job, conducting quality improvements, and achieving goals must be carefully managed so that the long-term effect of quality on the organization is a desirable one.

These costs must be a true measure of the quality effort, and they are best determined from an analysis of the costs of quality. Such an analysis provides a method of assessing the effectiveness of the management of quality and a means of determining problem areas, opportunities, savings, and action priorities.

Cost of quality is also an important communication tool. Philip Crosby demonstrated what a powerful tool it could be to raise awareness of the importance of quality. He referred to the measure as the "price of nonconformance" and argued that organizations choose to pay for poor quality. Many organizations will have true quality-related costs as high as 15-20% of sales revenue, some going as high as 40% of total operations. A general rule of thumb is that costs of poor quality in a thriving company will be about 10-15% of operations. Effective quality improvement programs can reduce this substantially, thus making a direct contribution to profits.

The quality cost system, once established, should become dynamic and have a positive impact on the achievement of the organization's mission, goals, and objection

MODULE III

TOOLS AND TECHNIQUES-1

Benchmarking, Information Technology, ISO 9000 Series of Quality Management Systems - Environmental Management Systems.

BENCHMARKING

Benchmarking is a systematic method by which organizations can measure themselves against the best industry practices.

Benchmarking is a systematic search for the best practices, innovative ideas, and highly effective operating procedures.

Fig: Benchmarking Concept

BENCHMARKING CONCEPT

```
┌─────────────────────────┐         ┌─────────────────────────┐
│ What is our performance │         │ What are others         │
│         level ?         │ ◄─────► │     performance levels ?│
│  • How do we do it ?    │         │  How did they get there?│
└─────────────────────────┘         └─────────────────────────┘
                 \                    /
                  \                  /
                   ( Creative Adaptation )
                            │
                            ▼
                 ┌─────────────────────────┐
                 │ Breakthrough Performance│
                 └─────────────────────────┘
```

Reasons to Benchmark:

- It is a tool to achieve business and competitive objectives.
- It can inspire managers (and Organizations) to compete.
- It is time and cost effective.

- It constantly scans the external environment to improve the process.
- Potential and useful technological breakthroughs can be located and adopted early.

THE BENCHMARKING PROCESS

The formal 10-step benchmarking process is shown in outline below.

1. PLANNING.

The essential steps are those of any plan development: what, who and how. Every function of an organization has or delivers a product or output.

Benchmarking is Appropriate for any output of a process or function, whether its a physical good, an order, a Shipment, an invoice, a service or a report.

To whom or what will we compare?

Business-to-business, direct competitors are certainly prime candidates to benchmark. But they are not the only targets. Benchmarking must be conducted against the best companies and business functions regardless of where they exist. How will the data be collected?

There is no one way to conduct benchmarking investigations. There is an infinite variety of ways to obtain required data – and most of the data you will need are readily and publicly available. Recognize that benchmarking is a process not only of deriving quantifiable goals and targets, but more importantly, it is the process of investigating and documenting the best industry practices, which can help you achieve goals and targets.

2. ANALYSIS.

The analysis phase must involve a careful understanding of your current process and practices, as well as those of the organizations being benchmarked. What is desired is an understanding of internal performance on which to assess strengths and weaknesses.

3. INTEGRATION.

Integration is the process of using benchmark findings to set operational targets for change. It involves careful planning to incorporate new practices in the operation and to ensure benchmark findings are incorporated in all formal planning processes. Gain operational and management acceptance of benchmark findings. Clearly and convincingly demonstrate findings as correct and based on substantive data. Develop action plans. Communicate findings to all organizational levels to obtain support, commitment, and ownership.

4. ACTION.

Convert benchmark findings, and operational principles based on them, to specific actions to be taken. Put in place a periodic measurement and assessment of achievement. Use the creative talents of the people who actually perform work tasks to determine how the findings can be incorporated into the work processes. Any plan for change also should contain milestones for updating the benchmark findings, and an ongoing reporting mechanism. Progress toward benchmark findings must be reported to all employees.

5. MATURITY.

Maturity will be reached when best industry practices are incorporated in all business processes, thus ensuring superiority. Maturity also is achieved when benchmarking becomes an ongoing, essential, and self-initiated facet of the management process. Benchmarking becomes institutionalized and is done at all appropriate levels of the organization, not by specialists.

Types of Benchmarking.

- Process benchmarking - the initiating firm focuses its observation and investigation of business processes with a goal of identifying and observing the best practices from one or more benchmark firms. Activity analysis will be required where the objective is to benchmark cost and efficiency; increasingly applied to back-office processes where outsourcing may be a consideration.

- Financial benchmarking - performing a financial analysis and comparing the results to assess your overall competitiveness.

- Performance benchmarking - allows the initiator firm to assess their competitive position by comparing products and services with those of target firms.

- Product benchmarking - the process of designing new products or upgrades to current ones. This process can sometimes involve reverse engineering which is taking apart competitors' products to find strengths and weaknesses.

- Strategic benchmarking - involves observing how others compete. This type is usually not industry specific meaning it is best to look at other industries.

- Functional benchmarking - a company will focus its benchmarking on a single function to improve the operation of that particular function. Complex functions such as Human Resources, Finance and Accounting and Information and Communication Technology are unlikely to be directly comparable in cost and efficiency terms and may need to be disaggregated into processes to make valid comparison.

INFORMATION TECHNOLOGY

Information technology for Total Quality Management has been significantly implemented on most organizations and each has been widely researched. Many organizations are providing better products and services with the help of introducing Information Technology in Total Quality Management. The global competition has enhanced the role of quality in business world whereas competition is adding to pressure to the organization. These challenges and pressures have placed a renewed focus on quality improvement for the long-term survival of the organization. Technology acts as an enabling mechanism, which results in enriched jobs and increased job satisfaction. TQM is a philosophy of management and asset for customer centric practices for delivering quality.

(IT) plays a critical role in Total Quality Management (TQM) by enabling organizations to implement, monitor, and continuously improve their quality management processes effectively.

Here's how IT supports TQM:

1. Data Collection and Analysis

- IT systems collect vast amounts of data related to processes, customer feedback, and performance metrics.

- Tools like data analytics software and dashboards help in identifying trends, inefficiencies, and areas for improvement.

2. Process Automation

    - Automating repetitive and manual tasks reduces errors and ensures consistency in quality processes.

    - IT facilitates faster and more reliable workflows, increasing efficiency.

3. Real-Time Monitoring

    - IT solutions like IoT sensors and ERP systems enable real-time tracking of production and operational processes.

    - Immediate alerts for deviations from quality standards ensure quick corrective actions.

4. Communication and Collaboration

    - IT fosters seamless communication across departments and locations through tools like cloud platforms and collaborative software.

    - Ensures that everyone is aligned with the organization's quality objectives.

5. Customer Relationship Management (CRM)

    - IT-based CRM systems help capture and analyse customer feedback, complaints, and preferences.

    - Enables organizations to tailor their offerings to enhance customer satisfaction.

6. Benchmarking and Best Practices

    - IT provides access to databases, reports, and case studies for benchmarking against industry standards.

    - Facilitates the adoption of best practices through e-learning and knowledge-sharing platforms.

7. Supply Chain Management

    - IT integrates supply chain operations, ensuring timely delivery and quality of inputs.

    - Reduces variability and enhances overall process efficiency.

8. Quality Control Tools

    - Statistical tools and software like SPC (Statistical Process Control) analyses process variations and maintain product quality.

    - Ensures compliance with quality standards.

9. Documentation and Compliance

    - IT systems streamline documentation of processes, policies, and compliance requirements.

    - Facilitates easy access and updates, ensuring adherence to quality standards like ISO 9001.

10. Continuous Improvement

    - IT supports continuous improvement by tracking progress, generating insights, and integrating customer feedback into quality initiatives.

- Tools like Six Sigma and Lean management software aid in process refinement.

The role of IT should even expand and increase more and more in manufacturing and industrial sector in particular in order for companies to enhance all different aspects of operations/processes.

ISO 9000 SERIES OF QUALITY MANAGEMENT SYSTEMS

Overview and Evolution

The International Organization of Standardization (ISO) was founded in 1946 in Geneva, Switzerland. The development of International Standards is to facilitate the exchange of goods and services worldwide. ISO consists of more than 90 country members. The ISO Technical Committee (TC) developed a series of International Standards for Quality Systems, which were first published in 1987. The standards (ISO 9000, 9001, and 9004) were intended to be advisory and developed for use in two-party contractual situations and internal auditing.

These standards were adopted by European Community and have been accepted worldwide with emphasis on quality and economic competitiveness. The fourth edition of ISO 9001 was released in the year 2008 and it replaces the third edition (ISO9001: 2000), which have been amended to clarify the points in the text and to enhance the compatibility with ISO 14001: 2004.

Most countries have adopted ISO 9000 series as their national standards.

Scope and Purpose

The ISO 9000 series Standards is generic in scope. By design, the series can be tailored to fit any organization's needs. Whether it is large or small, a manufacturer or a service organization. It can be applied to construction, engineering, health care, legal, and other professional services as well as the manufacturing of anything from nuts and bolts to spacecraft. Its purpose is to unify quality terms and definitions used by industrialized nations and use those terms to demonstrate the supplier's capability of controlling the processes. In very simplified terms, the standards require an organization to say what it is doing to ensure quality, then do what it says, and finally document or prove that it has done what it said.

The ISO 9000 Series of Standards.

- ISO 9000: 2005 - Quality Management Systems (QMS)

    Fundamentals and Vocabulary discusses the fundamental concepts related to QMS and provides the terminology used in the other two standards.

- ISO 9001: 2008 – Quality Management Systems (QMS)

    Requirements are the standards used registration by demonstrating conformity of the QMS to customers, regulatory and organization's own requirements.

- ISO 9004: 2000- Quality Management Systems (QMS)
- GUIDELINES FOR PERFORMANCE IMPROVEMENT provides guidelines that an organization can use to establish a QMS focused on improving performance.
- ISO 9001: Design, Development, Production, Installation & Servicing
- ISO 9002: Production, Installation & Servicing
- ISO 9003: Inspection & Testing
- ISO 9004: Provides guidelines on the technical, administrative and human factors affecting the product or services.

BENEFITS OF ISO 9000 STANDARDS:

- Achievement of international standard of quality.
- Value for money.
- Customer satisfaction.
- Higher productivity.
- Increased profitability
- Improved corporate image.
- Access to global market
- Growth of the organization
- Higher morale of employees

IS 14000 - ENVIRONMENTAL MANAGEMENT SYSTEMS (EMS)

The overall aim of the Environmental Management systems is to provide protection to the environment and to prevent pollution. The success of ISO 9000 along with increased emphasis on Environmental issues was instrumental in ISO's decision to develop Environmental Management Standards. In 1991, ISO formed the Strategic Advisory Group on the Environment (SAGE) which led to the formation of Technical Committee (TC) 207 in 1992. Mission of TC207 is to develop standards for an Environmental Management System (EMS) which was identified as ISO 14000.

TC 207 has Established six sub-committees.

- Environmental Management System (EMS)
- Environmental Auditing (EA)
- Environmental labelling (EL)

- Environmental Performance Evaluation (EPE)
- Life-Cycle Assessment (LCA)
- Terms & Definitions

REQUIREMENT OF ISO 14001

There are six elements:

1. GENERAL REQUIREMENTS

- EMS should include policy, planning implementation & operation, checking & corrective action, management review.

2. ENVIRONMENTAL POLICY (Should be based on mission)

- The policy must be relevant to the organization's nature.
- Management's Commitment (for continual improvement & preventing pollution).
- Should be a framework (for Environmental objectives & Targets).
- Must be Documented, Implemented, & Maintained.

3. PLANNING

- Environmental Aspects
- Legal & other Requirements
- Objectives & Targets
- Environmental Management Programs

4. IMPLEMENTATION & OPERATION

- Structure & Responsibility
- Training, Awareness & Competency
- Communication

- EMS Documentation
- Document Control
- Operational Control
- Emergency Preparedness & Response

5. CHECKING & CORRECTIVE ACTION

- Monitoring & Measuring
- Nonconformance & Corrective & Preventive action
- Records
- EMS Audit

6. MANAGENMENT REVIEW

- Review of objectives & targets
- Review of Environmental performance against legal & legal & another requirement [ ] Effectiveness of EMS elements
- Evaluation of the continuation of the policy

ISO 14000: Developed by Technical Committee TC 207 based on SAGE's recommendations.

Focuses on Environmental Management Systems (EMS) to manage the environmental impact of business activities, products, and services. Integrates environmental considerations into overall management practices for sustainable operations.

In summary, ISO 14000 complements ISO 9000 by emphasizing environmental responsibility alongside quality management.

ISO14000 is a generic standard. When we state the term generic, we mean that- like ISO9000it is not an industry specific standard.

The series is divided into two separate areas-the organization evaluation standards and the product evaluation standards. The first deals with Environmental Management System (EMS), Environmental Auditing (EA), and Environmental Performance Evaluation (EPE), whereas later deals with Environmental Aspects in Product Standards (EAPS), Environmental Labelling (EL), and Life Cycle Assessment (LCA).

Benefits of EMS:

GLOBAL BENEFITS

- Facilitate trade & remove trade barrier.
- Improve environmental performance of planet earth.
- Build consensus that there is a need for environmental management and a common terminology for EMS.

ORGANIZATIONAL BENEFITS

- Assuring customers of a commitment to environmental management.
- Meeting customer requirement.
- Improve public relation.
- Increase investor satisfaction Environmental Management System Model
- Market share increase
- Conserving input material & energy
- Better industry/government relation
- Low-cost insurance, easy attainment of permits & authorization

MODULE IV

TOOLS AND TECHNIQUES-2

QFD, FMEA, Quality Circles, TPM, Traditional Quality Tools and Management tools.

QUALITY FUNCTION DEPLOYMENT (QFD)

Quality Function Deployment (QFD) is a customer-driven approach to product and service design that focuses on translating customer requirements into specific engineering or operational specifications. Developed in Japan during the 1960s by Dr. Yoji Akao, QFD ensures that the voice of the customer (VoC) is systematically incorporated throughout the product development process.

Objectives of QFD:

- Customer-Centric Design: Ensure that products or services meet or exceed customer expectations.
- Improved Communication: Enhance collaboration between different teams and departments.
- Reduced Development Time: Minimize redesigns and delays by addressing customer needs upfront.
- Resource Optimization: Focus on features and processes that add value to the customer.

QFD Process:

The QFD process involves several steps to systematically translate customer requirements into actionable plans:

1. Identify Customer Requirements (CRs):

- Collect customer needs through surveys, interviews, or focus groups.
- Categorize and prioritize these needs based on their importance to the customer.

2. Develop the House of Quality (HoQ):

The House of Quality is a key tool in QFD that visually represents the relationship between customer requirements and technical specifications. It includes:

- Customer Requirements: What the customer wants.
- Technical Requirements: How the organization will meet these needs.
- Relationships Matrix: Correlates customer needs with technical solutions. Priorities: Assigns weights based on customer importance and feasibility.

3. Translate Requirements Across Functions:

- Each phase of the product lifecycle (design, production, marketing) uses the insights from HoQ to ensure alignment.
- Break down technical requirements into actionable steps for manufacturing, quality control, and other departments.

4. Benchmarking:

- Compare against competitors to identify gaps and opportunities for differentiation.

5. Develop and Test Prototypes:

- Use the technical specifications to create prototypes that meet customer expectations. ☐ Iterate based on customer feedback.

Figure 1 — House of quality template and benefits

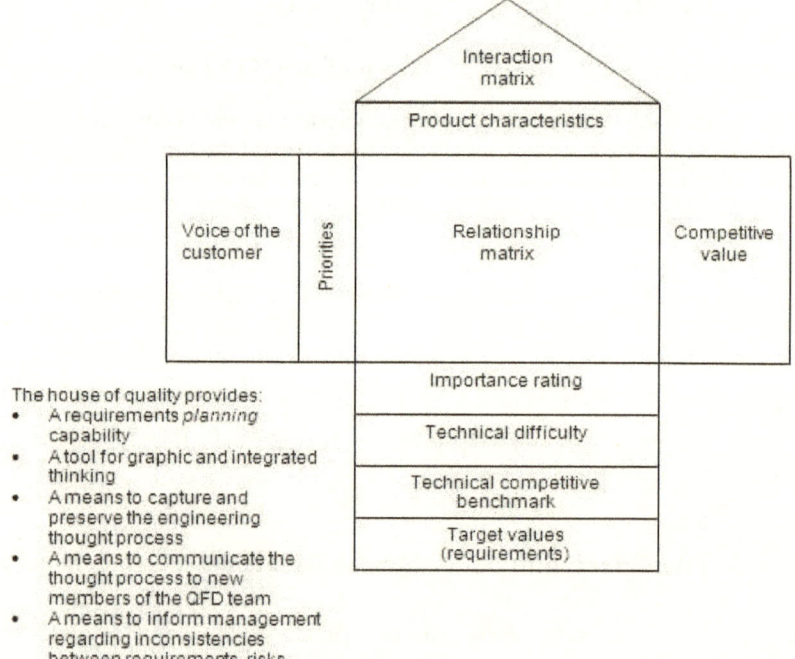

Fig: House of Quality

Benefits of QFD:

1. Improves Customer satisfaction

- Creates focus on customer requirements.
- Uses competitive information effectively.
- Prioritizes resources.
- Identifies items that can be acted upon

2. Reduces Implementation Time

- Decreases midstream design changes.
- Limits post introduction problems.
- Avoids future development redundancies.
- Promotes Teamwork.
- Creates communication.
- Identifies actions.

3. Provides Documentation

- Documents rationale for design.
- Adds structure to the information.
- Adapts to changes (a living document)

FAILURE MODE AND EFFECTS ANALYSIS (FMEA)

FMEA systematically identifies:

1. Failure Modes: How something might fail (e.g., defects in a product or errors in a process).

2. Effects: The impact of these failures on customers or system performance.

3. Causes: The underlying reasons for these failures.

FMEA is an analytical technique that combines the technology and experience of people inidentifying foreseeable failure modes of a product or process and planning for its elimination.FMEA is a "before-the-event" action requiring a team effort to alleviate changes easily and inexpensively in design and production.

It is a group of activities comprising the following:

- Recognize the potential failure of a product or process.
- Identify actions that eliminate / reduce the potential failure. ☐ Document the process.

Types of FMEA

FMEA can be applied at different stages and for various purposes:

1. Design FMEA (DFMEA)

- Focuses on potential failures in product design.
- Identifies design weaknesses before production.

2. Process FMEA (PFMEA)

- Analyses failures in manufacturing or assembly processes.
- Prevents process inefficiencies or defects.

3. System FMEA

- Evaluates failures at a higher system level, focusing on interactions between components.

4. Service FMEA

- Assesses potential failures in service delivery processes.

- Ensures customer satisfaction in service industries.

5. Software FMEA

- Identifies failures in software systems or algorithms.

FMEA Procedure

1. Define the Scope

- Purpose: Determine what product, process, or system you are analyzing.
- Actions:Clearly outline the boundaries of the analysis (e.g., design stage, manufacturing process, or service delivery).
- Define the goals of the FMEA (e.g., reduce defects, improve safety, enhance reliability).
- Identify key stakeholders.
- Example: For a car braking system, the scope might focus on the hydraulic mechanism.

2. Assemble a Team

- Purpose: Create a cross-functional team with relevant expertise.
- Actions:Include members from different departments (e.g., design, manufacturing, quality, and customer service).
- Ensure team members understand the product or process being analyzed.
- Assign roles and responsibilities for the FMEA study.
- Example: For a manufacturing FMEA, include engineers, operators, and quality assurance personnel.

3. List Potential Failure Modes

- Purpose: Identify all the possible ways the process or product could fail.
- Actions: Review historical data, such as defect reports or warranty claims.
- Brainstorm possible failure modes for each component or step in the process.
- Document failure modes in clear and specific terms.
- Example: In a production process, a potential failure mode could be "machine misalignment leading to defective parts."

4. Identify Effects and Severity

- Purpose: Assess the impact of each failure mode on the customer or system.
- Actions: Define the effects of each failure mode (e.g., safety risks, functionality loss).
- Rate the severity of the effect on a scale, typically from 1 (low) to 10 (high).
- Focus on customer impact when determining severity.
- Example: A failure in the car braking system might be rated 10 due to safety concerns.

5. Determine Causes and Occurrence

- Purpose: Identify the root causes of each failure mode and estimate how likely they are to occur.
- Actions: Use tools like Fishbone Diagrams (Ishikawa) or 5 Whys to find root causes.

- Rate the occurrence probability on a scale, usually from 1 (rare) to 10 (frequent).
- Example: A cause for defective parts might be "operator error due to lack of training."

6. **Identify Current Controls**
   - Purpose: Review existing mechanisms that prevent or detect failures.
   - Actions:List preventive controls (e.g., quality checks, error-proofing mechanisms).
   - List detection controls (e.g., inspections, alarms).
   - Rate the detection effectiveness on a scale, typically from 1 (very effective) to 10 (ineffective).
   - Example: A detection control might be "automated sensors to detect misaligned components."

7. **Calculate Risk Priority Number (RPN)**
   - Purpose: Prioritize failure modes based on their risk level.
   - Actions:Calculate RPN = Severity x Occurrence x Detection
   - Higher RPN values indicate more critical failure modes requiring immediate attention.
   - Rank the failure modes from highest to lowest RPN.

8. **Develop Action Plans**
   - Purpose: Create and implement strategies to address high-priority failure modes.
   - Actions:Propose corrective actions to reduce severity, occurrence, or improve detection.
   - Assign responsibilities to team members for executing the action plan.

- Document the proposed changes and expected outcomes.
- Example: Implementing additional operator training to reduce errors.

9. Implement and Monitor
   - Purpose: Apply corrective actions and assess their effectiveness.
   - Actions: Track the progress of the action plan and ensure timely implementation.
   - Reassess the RPN after implementing changes to confirm improvement.
   - Update FMEA documentation for future reference.
   - Example: After training, monitor error rates to ensure they have decreased.

BENEFITS OF FMEA IN TQM

- Proactive Problem Prevention: Anticipates potential failures and addresses them before they occur.
- Improved Quality and Reliability: Reduces defects and ensures robust product or process performance.
- Enhanced Customer Satisfaction: Minimizes the risk of customer-facing failures, improving trust and loyalty.
- Cost Reduction: Lowers costs by preventing rework, warranty claims, and recalls.
- Cross-Functional Collaboration: Encourages teamwork and knowledge sharing across departments.
- Systematic Risk Management: Provides a structured method to assess and mitigate risks.
- Continuous Improvement: Aligns with TQM principles by promoting ongoing enhancements in processes and designs.

- Regulatory Compliance: Helps meet industry standards and regulatory requirements for risk management.

QUALITY CIRCLES

A Quality Circle is a group of employees from the same work area or performing similar tasks who come together periodically to address quality, productivity, and other workplace issues. The focus is on collaborative problem-solving and contributing to organizational goals.

Objectives of a Quality Circle

- The primary objectives of Quality Circles are:
- Problem Solving: To identify and resolve quality issues, defects, or process inefficiencies.
- Continuous Improvement: To develop a culture of continuous improvement by encouraging employees to take ownership of quality-related challenges.
- Skill Development: To enhance the problem-solving, communication, and teamwork skills of participating employees.
- Increased Employee Engagement: Engaging employees in decision-making and quality improvement efforts leads to higher job satisfaction.

Structure of a Quality Circle

Quality Circles typically consist of the following elements:

- Team Members: Comprising 6-12 employees from various levels and departments of the organization.
- Team Leader: Facilitates meetings, ensures discussions stay on track, and acts as a liaison with management.

- Meetings: Regularly scheduled meetings where team members discuss and address quality issues.
- Problem-Solving Tools: Quality Circles use various problem-solving tools and techniques, such as the PDCA (Plan-Do-Check-Act) cycle and fishbone diagrams.

Quality is a cornerstone of success in today's competitive business landscape. Organizations employ various strategies and methodologies to achieve and maintain high standards of quality. One such approach is the use of Quality Circles, a dynamic and collaborative technique that empowers employees to participate in quality improvement initiatives actively. In this article, we will delve into what quality circles are, their objectives, the benefits they bring, their structure, and the processes they follow.

What Are Quality Circles?

Quality Circles, also known as QC or Kaizen Circles, are small groups of employees who voluntarily come together to identify, analyse, and solve quality-related problems within an organization. Originating in Japan in the 1960s, this concept has since spread worldwide as an effective means of improving quality and productivity.

Objectives of a Quality Circle

The primary objectives of Quality Circles are:

- Problem Solving: To identify and resolve quality issues, defects, or process inefficiencies.
- Continuous Improvement: To develop a culture of continuous improvement by encouraging employees to take ownership of quality-related challenges.

- Skill Development: To enhance the problem-solving, communication, and teamwork skills of participating employees.
- Increased Employee Engagement: Engaging employees in decision-making and quality improvement efforts leads to higher job satisfaction.

Benefits of Quality Circles

There are numerous benefits of Quality Circles:

- Improved Quality: QC teams are dedicated to finding and fixing quality issues, leading to better product or service quality.
- Cost Reduction: Organizations can reduce waste and operational costs by identifying and rectifying inefficiencies.
- Enhanced Employee Morale: Involvement in QC activities boosts employee morale, as they feel valued and engaged in making a difference.
- Higher Productivity: As QC teams tackle process bottlenecks, productivity increases, leading to more efficient operations.
- Innovation: QC teams often come up with innovative solutions to longstanding problems, driving organizational innovation.

Structure of a Quality Circle

Quality Circles typically consist of the following elements:

- Team Members: Comprising 6-12 employees from various levels and departments of the organization.
- Team Leader: Facilitates meetings, ensures discussions stay on track, and acts as a liaison with management.
- Meetings: Regularly scheduled meetings where team members discuss and address quality issues.

- Problem-Solving Tools: Quality Circles use various problem-solving tools and techniques, such as the PDCA (Plan-Do-Check-Act) cycle and fishbone diagrams.

Process of Quality Circles

Quality Circles follow a structured process:

- Identification of Problems: Team members identify quality-related problems and define their scope.
- Data Collection and Analysis: Data is gathered and analysed to understand the root cause of the problems.
- Generation of Solutions: The team brainstorms and generates potential solutions to the identified problems.
- Selection and Implementation: The best solution is chosen, and a plan is formulated for implementation.
- Review and Evaluation: The results of the solution's implementation are reviewed, and adjustments are made as needed.
- Standardization: Successful solutions are standardized into existing processes to ensure continuous improvement.

Benefits of Quality Circles

There are numerous benefits of Quality Circles:

- Improved Quality: QC teams are dedicated to finding and fixing quality issues, leading to better product or service quality.
- Cost Reduction: Organizations can reduce waste and operational costs by identifying and rectifying inefficiencies.

- Enhanced Employee Morale: Involvement in QC activities boosts employee morale, as they feel valued and engaged in making a difference.
- Higher Productivity: As QC teams tackle process bottlenecks, productivity increases, leading to more efficient operations.
- Innovation: QC teams often come up with innovative solutions to longstanding problems, driving organizational innovation.

Challenges in Quality Circles

- Lack of management support or buy-in.
- Inadequate training for team members.
- Resistance to change among employees.
- Poor communication between employees and management.

TOTAL PRODUCTIVE MAINTENANCE

TPM is a structured approach focused on optimizing the efficiency and reliability of equipment through a combination of maintenance, employee empowerment, and continuous improvement. It targets zero equipment failures, zero product defects, and zero accidents, aligning closely with the goals of TQM.

Key Principles of TPM

- Maximizing Equipment Effectiveness: Focus on achieving the highest performance by minimizing downtime, defects, and slow cycles.
- Involvement of All Employees: Engages operators, maintenance staff, and managers in maintenance activities.
- Proactive and Preventive Maintenance: Shifts from reactive maintenance to predictive and preventive practices.

- Continuous Improvement: Encourages ongoing efforts to enhance processes and eliminate inefficiencies.

TPM Pillars

TPM consists of eight pillars, each addressing specific aspects of equipment management and improvement:

1. Autonomous Maintenance:

- Operators take responsibility for basic maintenance tasks, such as cleaning, inspecting, and lubrication.
- Builds ownership and reduces dependency on specialized maintenance teams.

2. Planned Maintenance:

- Scheduled maintenance activities to prevent unexpected breakdowns.
- Involves using data to predict equipment failures and plan repairs proactively.

3. Focused Improvement:

- Cross-functional teams work on eliminating chronic issues and optimizing processes. ☐ Involves root cause analysis and innovative solutions.

4. Education and Training:

- Provide training to operators and maintenance personnel to improve their skills.
- Focus on technical knowledge, equipment handling, and maintenance techniques.

5. Early Equipment Management:

- Incorporate maintenance considerations during the design and installation of new equipment.
- Aims for easy maintenance and high reliability.

6. Quality Maintenance:

- Ensure that equipment consistently produces products of the desired quality.
- Involves identifying and eliminating equipment conditions that cause defects.

7. Office TPM:

- Apply TPM principles to administrative and office functions.
- Focus on reducing inefficiencies and improving workflows in non-production areas.

8. Safety, Health, and Environment:

- Foster a safe and healthy workplace by addressing risks associated with equipment and processes.
- Ensures compliance with environmental standards.

Benefits of TPM

- Enhanced Equipment Reliability: Reduces downtime and ensures smooth operations.
- Improved Product Quality: Minimizes defects by maintaining optimal machine conditions.
- Increased Productivity: Maximizes output through efficient processes.

- Cost Savings: Lowers repair costs and extends equipment lifespan.
- Employee Empowerment: Encourages ownership and responsibility among staff. Safety and Compliance: Reduces workplace accidents and ensures adherence to safety standards.
- Continuous Improvement: Promotes ongoing enhancements in maintenance and processes.
- Alignment with TQM: Supports organizational goals of quality and customer satisfaction.

TRADITIONAL QUALITY TOOLS AND MANAGEMENT TOOLS

Traditional Quality Tools and Management Tools are essential for identifying, analyzing, and solving quality-related issues. These tools are widely used in Total Quality Management (TQM) to facilitate decision-making, process control, and continuous improvement.

Traditional Quality Tools

The traditional seven quality tools were first identified by Kaoru Ishikawa and are often referred to as the "Seven Basic Tools of Quality." These tools are simple yet powerful for addressing quality challenges.

1. **Cause-and-Effect Diagram (Fishbone Diagram)**
    - Purpose: Identify the root causes of a problem.
    - Structure: A visual tool that categorizes potential causes under major headings (e.g., Man, Machine, Method, Material, Measurement, Environment).
    - Use Case: Analyse quality defects in a manufacturing process.

2. **Check Sheet**
   - Purpose: Collect and organize data systematically.
   - Structure: A form or table used to record occurrences of specific events or issues.
   - Use Case: Count the frequency of defects or monitor daily production.

3. **Control Chart**
   - Purpose: Monitor process stability and variability.
   - Structure: A graph that plots process data over time with upper and lower control limits.
   - Use Case: Determine if a process is operating within control limits.

4. **Histogram**
   - Purpose: Display the distribution of data.
   - Structure: A bar chart that shows frequency distribution.
   - Use Case: Identify patterns or deviations in data, such as product dimensions.

5. **Pareto Chart**
   - Purpose: Highlight the most significant issues affecting quality.
   - Structure: A bar graph where problems are ranked by frequency or impact. Use Case: Apply the 80/20 rule to focus on the critical few problems.

6. **Scatter Diagram**
   - Purpose: Show relationships between two variables.
   - Structure: A plot with one variable on the x-axis and another on the y-axis.

- Use Case: Analyse the correlation between machine speed and defect rates.

7. **Flowchart**
    - Purpose: Map out a process to identify inefficiencies.
    - Structure: A step-by-step diagram using symbols to represent activities, decisions, and flows.
    - Use Case: Visualize the workflow for quality inspection.

Management Tools

Management tools are designed to handle complex problems, facilitate decision-making, and support strategic planning. These tools go beyond operational-level issues and are often used for quality planning and improvement.

1. **Affinity Diagram**
    - Purpose: Organize large amounts of data or ideas into meaningful categories.
    - Use Case: Group feedback from brainstorming sessions into themes.

2. **Tree Diagram**
    - Purpose: Break down a goal or problem into actionable steps.
    - Structure: A hierarchical diagram starting with a broad objective and branching into details.
    - Use Case: Develop a step-by-step plan for achieving quality goals.

3. **Matrix Diagram**
    - Purpose: Show relationships between different variables or factors.

- Structure: A grid format with rows and columns to display connections.
- Use Case: Identify how customer requirements relate to product features.

4. **Prioritization Matrix**
   - Purpose: Rank options based on specific criteria.
   - Structure: A weighted matrix where alternatives are scored.
   - Use Case: Decide which quality improvement project to implement first.

5. **Process Decision Program Chart (PDPC)**
   - Purpose: Identify potential problems and countermeasures in a process.
   - Structure: A branching diagram showing possible risks and responses.
   - Use Case: Anticipate challenges in implementing new quality standards.

6. **Interrelationship Diagram**
   - Purpose: Understand cause-and-effect relationships between factors.
   - Structure: A network diagram with arrows indicating relationships.
   - Use Case: Analyse complex problems with multiple interdependencies.

7. **Activity Network Diagram (PERT/CPM Chart)**
   - Purpose: Plan and schedule project tasks.
   - Structure: A flowchart showing task dependencies, timelines, and critical paths. Use Case: Manage timelines for quality improvement initiatives.

Comparison: Traditional Quality Tools vs. Management Tools

Aspect	Traditional Quality Tools	Management Tools
Purpose	Operational-level problem-solving	Strategic planning and decision-making
Complexity	Simple, easy to use	Suitable for handling complex problems
Focus	Process control and improvement	Planning, prioritization, and relationship analysis
Example Tools	Control Chart, Pareto Chart, Fishbone Diagram	Affinity Diagram, Tree Diagram, Matrix Diagram

MODULE V

IMPLEMENTATION OF TQM

Steps in TQM implementation, national and international quality awards, case studies.

Implementing Total Quality Management (TQM) requires a structured and systematic approach to ensure that quality becomes an integral part of every business process. Below is a detailed elaboration of the **steps involved in TQM implementation:**

1. **Commitment from Top Management**
   - Leadership Role: The top management must demonstrate a strong commitment to quality by actively participating in TQM initiatives.
   - Set a Clear Vision: Define the organization's quality goals aligned with its mission and vision and communicate the importance of quality to all levels of the organization.
   - Resource Allocation: Ensure adequate resources (time, budget, and tools) are allocated for TQM activities.

2. **Create a TQM Steering Team**
   - Form the Team: Include representatives from different departments (e.g., production, quality, HR, and customer service). Ensure team members have diverse expertise to address various aspects of quality.
   - Define Responsibilities: Oversee the TQM implementation process and Develop action plans and monitor progress.

3. **Conduct Training and Awareness Programs**
   - Educate Employees: Train employees on TQM principles, tools, and techniques (e.g., Six Sigma, Kaizen, 5S). Provide specific training for roles related to quality control and assurance.
   - Promote Awareness: Use workshops, seminars, and communication channels to emphasize the importance of quality. Foster a culture where employees understand their role in maintaining quality.

4. **Identify and Understand Customer Needs**
   - Gather Feedback: Conduct surveys, interviews, and focus groups to understand customer expectations.
   - Analyse complaints and feedback to identify areas for improvement.
   - Define Quality Goals: Translate customer needs into measurable objectives. Prioritize critical areas that directly impact customer satisfaction.

5. **Assess the Current Processes**
   - Map Existing Processes: Document workflows and identify key processes affecting quality. Use tools like flowcharts and process diagrams for visualization.
   - Evaluate Performance: Analyse current process efficiency using metrics like defect rates, cycle times, and productivity. Identify gaps and inefficiencies in processes.

6. **Develop a TQM Implementation Plan**
   - Set Objectives: Define short-term and long-term quality improvement goals. Ensure goals are SMART (Specific, Measurable, Achievable, Relevant, Time-bound).

- Plan Activities: Outline specific steps to improve quality, such as introducing quality control measures or adopting new tools. Set timelines and assign responsibilities to team members.

7. **Use Quality Tools and Techniques**
   - Traditional Tools: Apply tools like Control Charts, Pareto Analysis, and Fishbone Diagrams for problem-solving.
   - Advanced Techniques: Use Six Sigma, Statistical Process Control (SPC), and Failure Mode and Effects Analysis (FMEA) for data-driven decision-making.
   - Monitor Processes: Continuously track performance using Key Performance Indicators (KPIs).

8. **Focus on Continuous Improvement**
   - Adopt Kaizen: Encourage small, incremental changes for process improvement. Engage employees at all levels to contribute ideas.
   - Implement PDCA Cycle

9. **Foster Employee Involvement**
   - Empower Employees: Encourage employees to take ownership of quality initiatives. Provide tools and resources for effective participation.
   - Recognize Contributions: Reward and acknowledge employees' efforts in quality improvement.

10. **Build Strong Supplier Partnerships**
    - Collaborate with Suppliers: Share quality expectations and provide training for suppliers. Develop long-term relationships to ensure consistent quality of raw materials and components.
    - Monitor Supplier Performance: Regularly assess supplier quality through audits and evaluations.

11. **Measure Performance**
    - Establish Metrics: Use KPIs to evaluate the effectiveness of quality initiatives. Monitor metrics such as defect rates, customer satisfaction scores, and process efficiency.
    - Analyze Data: Identify trends and areas needing improvement using tools like dashboards and data analytics.

12. Conduct Reviews and Audits
    - Periodic Reviews: Hold regular meetings to review the progress of TQM initiatives. Assess whether goals and objectives are being met.
    - Audits: Conduct internal and external audits to ensure compliance with quality standards like ISO 9001. Use audit findings to refine processes.

13. **Standardize Best Practices**
    - Document Improvements: Record successful quality practices and integrate them into standard operating procedures (SOPs).
    - Ensure Consistency: Train employees to follow standardized processes to maintain uniform quality.

14. **Celebrate Achievements**
    - Recognize Milestones: Celebrate accomplishments to boost morale and reinforce commitment to quality.
    - Share Success Stories: Use case studies and reports to demonstrate the benefits of TQM to employees and stakeholders.

15. **Sustain the TQM Culture**
    - Leadership Support: Continuously engage leaders in promoting and supporting quality initiatives.

- Continuous Monitoring: Regularly revisit quality objectives and adjust strategies to align with changing business needs.
- Employee Engagement: Keep employees motivated and involved in quality improvement activities.

1. NATIONAL AND INTERNATIONAL QUALITY AWARDS

Quality awards play a significant role in recognizing organizations that have demonstrated excellence in Total Quality Management (TQM). These awards provide a benchmark for best practices and encourage continuous improvement. Below is an overview of major **national and international quality awards**.

1. International Quality Awards

a. **Deming Prize (Japan)**
- Established: 1951 by the Union of Japanese Scientists and Engineers (JUSE). Purpose: To recognize organizations for their outstanding TQM practices.
- Criteria: Strategic use of TQM principles. Results in quality improvement and customer satisfaction.
- Eligibility: Open to organizations worldwide.

b. **Malcolm Baldrige National Quality Award (MBNQA) (USA)**
- Established: 1987 by the U.S. Congress.
- Purpose: To promote excellence in organizational performance and TQM.
- Criteria: Leadership, strategic planning, customer focus, measurement, workforce, operations, and results.

- Eligibility: U.S. organizations in sectors like manufacturing, healthcare, education, and non-profits.

c. **European Foundation for Quality Management (EFQM) Excellence Award**
- Established: 1991 by the EFQM Foundation.
- Purpose: To recognize European organizations for excellence through a holistic approach to management.
- Criteria: Leadership, people, processes, partnerships, and business results. □ Eligibility: European organizations from various industries.

d. **ISO Awards for Excellence**
- Established: By the International Organization for Standardization (ISO).
- Purpose: To recognize organizations that meet and exceed global standards like ISO 9001 and ISO 14001.
- Criteria: Consistency in quality management and environmental standards.

e. **Asia Pacific Quality Organization (APQO) Global Performance Excellence Award**
- Purpose: To recognize world-class organizations in the Asia-Pacific region for achieving excellence in quality and performance.
- Criteria: Focus on leadership, strategy, and operational excellence.

2 National Quality Awards

a. **Rajiv Gandhi National Quality Award (India)**
- Established: 1991 by the Bureau of Indian Standards (BIS).

- Purpose: To recognize Indian organizations for excellence in quality management.
- Criteria: TQM practices, employee involvement, and customer satisfaction.
- Eligibility: Manufacturing, service, and small business sectors in India.

b. **CII-EXIM Bank Award for Business Excellence (India)**
- Purpose: To encourage Indian organizations to adopt excellence models and achieve world-class performance.
- Criteria: Leadership, policy, strategy, and performance results.
- Eligibility: Indian companies in various sectors.

c. **Shingo Prize for Operational Excellence (USA) Established: By Utah State University.**
- Purpose: Recognizes operational excellence, including lean practices and continuous improvement.
- Criteria: Cultural enablers, continuous process improvement, and results.

d. **Australian Business Excellence Awards**
- Established: By the Australian Organizational Excellence Foundation.
- Purpose: To acknowledge Australian organizations with outstanding quality practices.
- Criteria: Leadership, strategy, customer focus, and results. Eligibility: Open to all Australian organizations.

e. **Canada Awards for Excellence Established: By Excellence Canada.**
- Purpose: To honour Canadian organizations that demonstrate excellence in quality and innovation.

- Criteria: Commitment to excellence, customer focus, and innovation.
- National Quality Award of Brazil (PNQ)
- Established: By the Brazilian National Quality Foundation (FNQ).
- Purpose: To promote the adoption of quality management models in Brazil.
- Criteria: Leadership, strategy, results, and innovation.

Benefits of Quality Awards in TQM

- Recognition: Highlights organizations that excel in implementing TQM practices.
- Benchmarking: Provides a standard for other organizations to emulate.
- Continuous Improvement: Encourages the adoption of innovative practices.
- Customer Confidence: Builds trust and confidence among customers.
- Employee Motivation: Recognizes the efforts of employees, boosting morale and engagement.

Few Case Studies about TQM

1. TOYOTA: THE PIONEER OF TQM

Background: Toyota is a global leader in the automobile industry and is known for its commitment to quality through its Toyota Production System (TPS).

TQM Practices:

Kaizen: Continuous improvement involving employees at all levels.

- Just-In-Time (JIT): Reducing waste by producing only what is needed when needed.
- Jidoka: Automation with a human touch—machines stop automatically when an issue arises.
- Customer Focus: Rigorous attention to customer feedback and requirements.

Results:

- High-quality vehicles with minimal defects. ☐ Enhanced customer satisfaction and loyalty.
- Global recognition for reliability and innovation.

2 MOTOROLA: BIRTHPLACE OF SIX SIGMA

Background: In the 1980s, Motorola faced challenges with product defects and customer dissatisfaction.

TQM Practices:

Six Sigma: Introduced as a methodology to reduce defects and improve quality.

- Employee Training: Extensive training programs on quality tools and Six Sigma techniques.
- Customer-Centric Approach: Focused on understanding customer needs and expectations.

Results:

- Reduced defects to less than 3.4 per million opportunities.
- Cost savings of over $16 billion in a decade.
- Improved brand reputation and customer trust.

3. XEROX CORPORATION: FROM CRISIS TO QUALITY LEADER

Background: Xerox faced intense competition in the 1980s, leading to declining market share and profitability.

TQM Practices:

- Benchmarking: Xerox identified best practices from industry leaders and applied them.
- Leadership Commitment: Strong support from top management for TQM initiatives.
- Employee Empowerment: Encouraged employees to participate in quality improvement programs.

Results:

- Reduction in manufacturing costs by 50%.
- Increased customer satisfaction and regained market leadership.
- Won the Malcolm Baldrige National Quality Award in 1989.

4. COCA-COLA: ENSURING PRODUCT CONSISTENCY

Background: Coca-Cola implemented TQM to maintain product quality and consistency across global markets.

TQM Practices:

- Quality Control Systems: Standardized processes for manufacturing and bottling. ☐ Supplier Partnerships: Collaborated with suppliers to ensure raw material quality.
- Consumer Insights: Used feedback to refine products and services.

Results:

- Consistent taste and quality of products worldwide.
- Increased customer loyalty and brand strength.
- Operational efficiency and cost savings.

5. INFOSYS: QUALITY IN IT SERVICES

Background: Infosys is a global leader in IT services and adopted TQM to enhance service delivery.

TQM Practices:

- CMMI Framework: Implemented Capability Maturity Model Integration (CMMI) for software quality.
- Customer Collaboration: Close collaboration with clients to meet specific needs.
- Knowledge Management: Robust systems for sharing knowledge and best practices.

Results:

- Improved software quality and client satisfaction.
- Recognition as a trusted partner for global IT solutions. ⌂ Consistent business growth and awards for excellence. Key Learnings from Case Studies
- Leadership is Essential: Strong commitment from top management drives TQM success.
- Employee Involvement Matters: Engaging employees in quality initiatives leads to better results.

- Focus on Customers: TQM practices should prioritize customer satisfaction and loyalty.
- Continuous Improvement: Regularly revisiting and refining processes is crucial.
- Use of Quality Tools: Tools like Six Sigma, Kaizen, and benchmarking are effective for achieving excellence.

MODULE VI
INTRODUCTION TO MANEGEMENT ECONOMIC

The themes of Ergonomics – scarcity and efficiency – three fundamental economic problems – society's capability – Production possibility frontiers (PPF) – Productive efficiency Vs economic efficiency – economic growth & stability – Micro economies and Macro economies – the role of markets and government – Positive Vs negative externalities.

Businesses face critical decisions daily, ranging from investment opportunities and launching new products to tackling emerging competitors and determining the company's overall direction. To navigate these challenges effectively, managerial Ergonomics equips managers with essential tools and techniques. These include analyzing market demand, assessing costs, setting pricing strategies, evaluating risks, and understanding competitive dynamics, enabling well-informed decision-making.

Managerial Ergonomics is a stream of management studies that focuses on solving business problems and making decisions by applying the theories & principles of micro-Ergonomics & macro-Ergonomics.

Managerial Ergonomics serves as a bridge between economic theory and practical business applications, focusing on maximizing efficiency and profitability. It provides a systematic approach to assess the monetary value of various opportunities, guiding businesses in prioritizing investments and strategies. By integrating economic concepts with quantitative methods, managerial Ergonomics helps managers address complex problems with clarity and precision.

The concept of the nature of managerial Ergonomics includes the following:

1. Art and Science

Management theory requires a lot of critical and logical thinking and analytical skills to make decisions or solve problems. Many economists also find it a source of research, saying it includes applying different economic concepts, techniques, and methods to solve business problems.

2. MicroErgonomics

Managers typically deal with problems relevant to a single entity rather than the economy as a whole. It is, therefore, considered an integral part of microErgonomics.

3. Uses of Macro Ergonomics

A corporation works in an external world, i.e., serving the consumer, an important part of the economy. For this purpose, managers must evaluate the various macroeconomic factors, such as market dynamics, economic changes, government policies, etc., and their effect on the company.

4. Multidisciplinary

Managerial Ergonomics uses many tools and principles that belong to different disciplines, such as accounting, finance, statistics, mathematics, production, operational research, human resources, marketing, etc.

5. Prescriptive or Normative Discipline

By introducing corrective steps, managerial Ergonomics aims to achieve its objective and solves specific issues or problems.

6. Management Oriented

This serves as an instrument for managers to deal effectively with business-related problems and uncertainties. This also allows for setting priorities, formulating policies, and making successful decisions.

7. Pragmatic

The solution to day-to-day business challenges is realistic and rational. Different individuals take different views of the principles of managerial Ergonomics. Others may concentrate more on customer service and prioritize efficient production.

THEMES OF ERGONOMICS

The themes within managerial Ergonomics revolve around several key concepts that are essential for the efficient functioning of a firm. Here are some prominent themes:

1. Optimization and Decision Making

At the heart of managerial Ergonomics is the concept of optimization, where managers aim to maximize profits, minimize costs, or achieve some other objective. Decision-making tools such as marginal analysis (analyzing the impact of small changes in variables) and cost-benefit analysis are central to this theme. Managers must evaluate trade-offs, considering both short term and long-term impacts.

2. Demand and Supply Analysis

Understanding how demand and supply influence market prices and quantities is a key theme. This includes understanding consumer behavior (demand) and the factors that affect the production costs and availability of goods (supply). Managers need to analyze market conditions and customer preferences to set appropriate prices, adjust production levels, and identify profitable opportunities.

3. Production and Cost Analysis

Another critical theme is determining the optimal level of production and understanding the associated costs. This includes analyzing short-run and long-run cost structures, economies of scale, and the production function. Managers use these insights to find the most efficient combination of inputs (labor, capital, materials) to minimize costs while meeting demand.

4. Market Structure and Competitive Strategy

The market structure (e.g., perfect competition, monopoly, oligopoly) plays a significant role in shaping managerial strategies. Managers need to assess the competitive environment and develop strategies accordingly, whether it's pricing strategies in an oligopoly or differentiation strategies in a monopoly. The theme involves studying pricing power, barriers to entry, and product differentiation.

5. Pricing and Pricing Strategies

Pricing is a crucial theme in managerial Ergonomics, as it directly affects profitability. Managers must understand how to set prices based on demand elasticity, competitor pricing, and production costs. Different pricing strategies such as price discrimination, penetration pricing, skimming pricing, and bundling are used to optimize revenue and market share.

6. Risk and Uncertainty

Managers often make decisions under conditions of uncertainty. This theme involves applying risk analysis and decision-making models to handle situations where future outcomes are unknown. Techniques such as expected value, decision trees, and probabilistic risk assessment are employed to make informed decisions in uncertain environments.

7. Labor and Capital Markets

Labor Ergonomics is a theme that looks at how wages, employment, and productivity are determined. Managers need to make decisions regarding compensation, training, and workforce optimization. Similarly, capital market analysis is important for decisions regarding financing and capital structure.

8. Government Policies and Regulations

Managers must also be aware of government intervention in markets, including taxes, subsidies, antitrust regulations, and labor laws. The impact of these policies on cost structures, pricing, and profitability is a central theme in managerial Ergonomics. Firms must navigate regulatory frameworks while aligning their strategies to achieve organizational goals.

9. Environmental and Sustainability Considerations

In recent years, sustainability has become a key theme. Managers are increasingly considering the environmental and social impacts of their decisions. This includes evaluating externalities (positive and negative), sustainable production practices, and adapting to climate change policies. Firms are exploring how to balance economic goals with environmental responsibility.

SCARCITY AND EFFICIENCY IN MANAGERIAL ERGONOMICS

In managerial Ergonomics, scarcity and efficiency are interconnected:

- Scarcity forces firms to be efficient because they can't afford to waste resources. Limited resources compel businesses to focus on efficiency to remain competitive and profitable.

- Efficiency helps firms mitigate scarcity by maximizing the use of available resources, ensuring that every unit of input contributes as much as possible to output.

For instance, a company that faces a shortage of skilled labor must find ways to improve labor efficiency—either by investing in training or adopting technology to make better use of existing employees. Alternatively, if there's a shortage of raw materials, a firm might seek alternative suppliers or innovate to use fewer materials without compromising quality.

Managers must constantly balance **scarcity and efficiency**, making decisions that optimize the use of resources while addressing the trade-offs that come with limited availability. The goal is always to maximize the firm's profitability while responding to market forces and consumer demand.

Scarcity refers to the basic economic problem that resources (such as labor, capital, land, and raw materials) are limited, while human wants and business needs are virtually unlimited. In the context of managerial Ergonomics, scarcity requires managers to make decisions about how to allocate these limited resources effectively.

- Resource Allocation: Managers must decide how to allocate resources across different production processes, ensuring they use them in the most productive way to meet market demand. This involves choosing between different uses for resources, each of which has its own opportunity cost (the value of the next best alternative that must be forgone).
- Opportunity Cost: When faced with scarcity, every decision comes with an opportunity cost. For example, if a

manager chooses to use capital to expand a factory, the opportunity cost could be the foregone investment in new technology. Understanding opportunity cost helps managers make more informed decisions and prioritize investments that maximize value.

- Trade-offs: Scarcity forces businesses to make trade-offs. For instance, a firm may face the decision of whether to produce more of one product at the cost of producing less of another. In these situations, managers need to evaluate which option provides the greatest benefit or utility, given the constraints they face.

- Demand and Supply: Scarcity affects both demand and supply in the market. If a good or service is scarce, its price tends to rise due to increased demand or limited availability. Conversely, if resources for production are scarce, firms may face higher production costs, which can influence pricing and profitability.

Efficiency

Efficiency refers to how well a firm uses its resources to achieve its goals. In the context of managerial Ergonomics, efficiency is crucial for optimizing output, minimizing costs, and maximizing profits. There are two key types of efficiency relevant to managerial Ergonomics.

a) Allocative Efficiency

Allocative efficiency occurs when resources are distributed in a way that maximizes the overall benefit to society and the firm. In business, it refers to the allocation of resources to produce the combination of goods and services that consumers most desire, at the right price.

b) Productive Efficiency

Productive efficiency is achieved when a firm produces its goods or services at the lowest possible cost. This involves minimizing waste and maximizing output given the resources available.

1. What are the Fundamental Economic Problems?

In managerial Ergonomics, three fundamental economic problems shape the decisions that firms must make. These problems arise from the basic economic principle that resources are scarce, but human wants and needs are virtually unlimited. The three key economic problems are: 1. What to Produce?

This problem involves deciding which goods and services a firm should produce, given its limited resources. For a business, the choices can range from deciding which products to manufacture to which services to offer in order to meet market demand.

- Demand Analysis: Managers need to understand what products consumers want most, how much they are willing to pay for them, and how to cater to market preferences. Conducting market research, analyzing consumer behavior, and studying trends are essential to answering this question.
- Profit Maximization: Firms must also consider profitability in deciding what to produce. Products that have high demand but low production costs tend to offer higher profits, so managers need to evaluate potential return on investment (ROI) for different product lines.
- Opportunity Cost: Choosing one product means sacrificing the production of another. The opportunity cost (the value of the next best alternative) of producing one good

over another must be carefully considered to optimize resource use.

2. How to Produce?

This question focuses on determining the most efficient method of production, given the available resources. It involves decisions about the combination of inputs (such as labor, capital, and materials) that will lead to the lowest cost while achieving the desired level of output.

   a. Cost Efficiency: Managers must assess which combination of labor, capital, and technology is most cost-effective. For instance, should a firm rely on human labor or automation? How can production processes be streamlined to minimize waste and reduce costs? This is where concepts like marginal cost and economies of scale come into play.

   b. Technology and Innovation: Firms often need to choose between different technological options to produce goods or services more efficiently. Innovation can help achieve productive efficiency, allowing firms to produce more output with fewer resources.

   c. Sustainability Considerations: Increasingly, firms must also consider the environmental impact of their production methods. Managers may need to choose production processes that are both cost-effective and sustainable, ensuring long-term viability without harming the environment.

3. For Whom to Produce?

This problem addresses the distribution of goods and services once they have been produced. It essentially involves deciding which consumers or market segments will receive the goods or services, and at what price.

a. Market Segmentation and Targeting: Firms must identify the target market that can afford and is willing to pay for their products. This may involve segmenting the market based on income, geographic location, consumer preferences, and other factors. The goal is to match the right product to the right consumer group.

b. Pricing Strategy: The price at which goods and services are sold is a key factor in determining who can afford them. Managers must decide on pricing strategies (e.g., penetration pricing, price skimming, or price discrimination) to maximize sales and profits while catering to the right consumer segments.

c. Income Distribution: Managers must also consider the purchasing power of different groups in society. For example, luxury products may be targeted at high-income consumers, while affordable products are aimed at lower-income groups. Understanding income distribution helps firms set prices and produce in a way that maximizes overall market reach.

Interconnection of the Three Problems

These three fundamental economic problems are highly interconnected:

a. The choice of what to produce affects the production methods (how to produce), as different products require different resources and technologies.
b. The method of production will determine the cost structure, which impacts how the firm can price its goods or services and, therefore, who can afford to buy them.
c. Additionally, the distribution of goods influences future decisions on what to produce—if a firm knows that a

particular market segment is willing to pay more for a product, it may shift resources to cater to that demand.

Society's capability refers to the broader economic, social, and institutional environment that influences a firm's decision-making process. It encompasses the availability of resources (labor, capital, raw materials, and technology), which directly impacts production costs and innovation potential. A society's infrastructure—including transportation, financial institutions, and legal systems—also plays a key role in shaping how efficiently businesses can operate and access capital.

Market conditions and consumer demand are vital, as firms must align production with what consumers want, and the level of competition affects pricing and resource allocation. Additionally, growing attention to environmental and social responsibility forces firms to consider sustainability, ethical sourcing, and corporate social responsibility (CSR) as part of their strategies.

A society's capacity for innovation and entrepreneurship fosters new business ventures and technological advancements, while global economic integration exposes firms to international markets and supply chains, expanding opportunities but also introducing risks. Ultimately, societal factors such as economic growth, regulatory frameworks, and technological development shape the strategies that managers adopt to remain competitive and efficient in an ever-changing business landscape.

PRODUCTION POSSIBILITY FRONTIERS

The production possibility frontier (PPF) is a curve on a graph that illustrates the possible quantities that can be produced of two products if both depend upon the same finite resource for their manufacture. The PPF is also referred to as the production possibility curve.

PPF also plays a crucial role in Ergonomics. For example, it can demonstrate that a nation's economy has reached the highest level of efficiency possible.

Key Takeaways

- When producing goods, opportunity cost is what is given up when you take resources from one product to produce another. The maximum amount that can be produced is illustrated by a curve on a graph.
- The production possibility frontier (PPF) is above the curve, illustrating impossible scenarios given the available resources.
- The PPF demonstrates that the production of one commodity may increase only if the production of the other commodity decreases.
- The PPF is a decision-making tool for managers deciding on the optimum product mix for the company.

The PPF is the area on a graph representing production levels that cannot be obtained given the available resources; the curve represents optimal levels. Here are the assumptions involved:

- A company/economy wants to produce two products.
- There are limited resources.
- Technology and techniques remain constant. All resources are fully and efficiently used.

If a company is deciding how much of each product to produce, it can plot points on a graph representing the number of products made using variables based on amounts of available resources. Considering that resources are limited, if the desire is to produce more of one product, resources must be taken away from the other.

The PPF is the area on a graph representing production levels that cannot be obtained given the available resources; the curve represents optimal levels. Here are the assumptions involved:

- A company/economy wants to produce two products.
- There are limited resources.
- Technology and techniques remain constant.
- All resources are fully and efficiently used.

If a company is deciding how much of each product to produce, it can plot points on a graph representing the number of products made using variables based on amounts of available resources. Considering that resources are limited, if the desire is to produce more of one product, resources must be taken away from the other.

Fig: PPF Curve

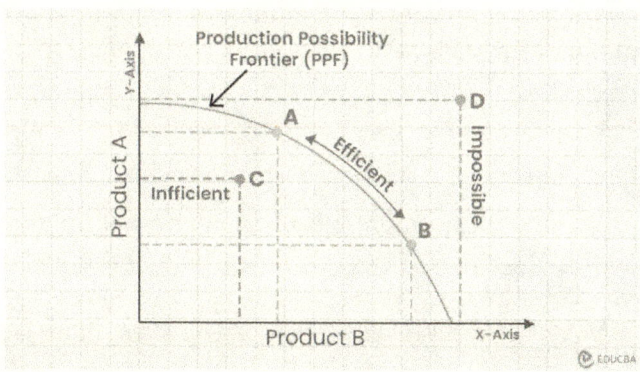

For an Economy: This technique can be used by economists to determine the set of points at which a country's economy is most efficiently allocating its resources to produce as many goods as possible. If the production level is on the curve, the country can only produce more of one good if it produces less of some other good.

If the economy is producing less than the quantities indicated by the curve, this signifies that resources are not being used to their full potential. In this case, it is possible to increase the production of some goods without cutting production in other areas. The production possibility frontier demonstrates that there are limits on production, given that the assumptions hold. Therefore, each economy must decide what combination of goods and services should be produced to attain maximum resource efficiency.

The Production Possibility Frontier provides a visual representation of an economy's constraints, choices, and trade-offs. It helps explain the relationship between resource allocation, efficiency, and opportunity cost, and is an essential tool for understanding economic decision-making.

PRODUCTION EFFICIENCY V/S ERGONOMICS EFFICIENCY

1. Production Efficiency

- Definition: Achieving the maximum output from a given set of inputs (or achieving a specific output with the minimum inputs). It ensures there is no wastage in the production process.
- Focus: Minimizing technical inefficiency.
- Key Characteristics:
    - Occurs on the production possibility frontier (PPF), where all resources are fully utilized.

- It does not consider the cost of inputs or whether the chosen combination is the most economical.
- Example: A factory that produces 500 units of output using the minimum possible labor and materials is production-efficient.

2. Economic Efficiency

- Definition: Achieving the production of goods or services at the lowest possible cost, considering both input costs and consumer preferences.
- Focus: Balancing both allocative efficiency and productive efficiency to maximize societal welfare.

- Key Characteristics:
  - Takes into account the opportunity cost of resources. Aligns production with market demand to avoid overproduction or underproduction.
  - Example: A company produces 500 units using not only minimal inputs but also the least-cost combination of inputs, ensuring profitability and meeting consumer demand.

Economic growth and **economic stability** are two critical goals in managerial Ergonomics and macroeconomic policy. They are interconnected but distinct concepts, each playing a vital role in shaping a country's economic health and business environment.

Aspect	Production Efficiency	Economic Efficiency
Focus	Technical optimization	Cost-effectiveness and resource allocation
Scope	Purely operational	Broader, includes consumer preferences and opportunity costs
Relevance to Decision-Making	Internal processes and waste reduction	Pricing, resource allocation, and meeting demand
Outcome	Maximum output with given inputs	Optimal output at minimal cost, aligned with demand

Economic Growth

- Definition: The increase in the production of goods and services in an economy over a period of time, typically measured by the rise in Gross Domestic Product (GDP) or Gross National Product (GNP).
- Focus: Expanding the economy's productive capacity and output.

Economic Stability

- Definition: A state in which an economy operates smoothly without large fluctuations in output, employment, and prices. Stability ensures sustainable growth and minimizes the risks of economic crises.
- Focus: Maintaining balance in key economic indicators like inflation, unemployment, and exchange rates.

Interconnection between Growth and Stability

1. Mutual Reinforcement:

- Economic growth can contribute to stability by increasing income, employment, and government revenues, which can be used to manage volatility.

- Stability, in turn, fosters an environment where businesses can invest and grow without fear of unexpected economic shocks.

2. Trade-Offs:

- Rapid economic growth can sometimes undermine stability, especially if it leads to inflation, asset bubbles, or resource overutilization.
- Over-prioritizing stability might suppress growth if restrictive policies (e.g., high interest rates) are imposed to control inflation.

To understand why both microeconomic and macroeconomic perspectives are useful, consider the problem of studying a biological ecosystem like a lake. One person who sets out to study the lake might focus on specific topics: certain kinds of algae or plant life; the characteristics of particular fish or snails; or the trees surrounding the lake. Another person might take an overall view and instead consider the lake's ecosystem from top to bottom; what eats what, how the system stays in a rough balance, and what environmental stresses affect this balance. Both approaches are useful, and both examine the same lake, but the viewpoints are different. In a similar way, both microErgonomics and macroErgonomics study the same economy, but each has a different viewpoint.

Whether you are scrutinizing lakes or Ergonomics, the micro and the macro insights should blend with each other. In studying a lake, the micro insights about particular plants and animals help to understand the overall food chain, while the macro insights about the overall food chain help to explain the environment in which individual plants and animals live. In Ergonomics, the micro decisions of individual businesses are influenced by whether the macro-economy is healthy.

MICROERGONOMICS

Definition: MicroErgonomics is the study of individuals, households and firms' behaviour in decisions making and allocation of resources. It generally applies to markets of goods and services and deals with individual and economic issues.

- MicroErgonomics is a branch of Ergonomics that studies the behaviour of individuals and firms in making decisions regarding the allocation of scarce resources and the interactions among these individuals and firms.

Microeconomic study deals with what choices people make, what factors influence their choices and how their decisions affect the goods markets by affecting the price, the supply and demand.

- One goal of microErgonomics is to analyze the market mechanisms that establish relative price among goods and services and allocate limited resources among alternative uses.
- MicroErgonomics shows condition under which free markets lead to desirable allocations. It also analyzes market failure, where markets fail to produce efficient results.

Importance of Micro- Economic Analysis

- Allocation of resources
- The distribution of national income

- Consideration of welfare
- Importance of applied field of Ergonomics

Limitation of Micro- Economic Analysis

- It always thinks of individual factors of production or individual consumer so it may not be always true on aggregate levels.
- Its result or conclusions are always on certain assumption.
- The aggregate analysis or the overall approach to any economic problem is beyond the reach of it.

MACROERGONOMICS

Definition: MacroErgonomics is a part of economic study which analyzes the economy as a whole. It is the average of the entire economy and does not study any individual unit or a firm. It studies the national income, total employment, aggregate demand and supply etc.

- MacroErgonomics is the study of the performance, structure, behaviour and decision-making of an economy as a whole. It focus on the national, regional, and global scales to maximize national income and provide national economic growth.
- The term 'Macro' has been derived from a Greek word 'Macros' meaning 'large'. Thus Macro- Ergonomics is the study and analysis of an economy as a whole.
  - Macroeconomists focus on the national, regional and global scales

- For most macroeconomists the purpose of this discipline is to maximize national income and provide national economic growth.
- This growth further increases utility and improve standard of living for the economy's participants.

Importance of Macro- economic Analysis:

- It never neglect the relationship between demand & supply as in case of micro- economic analysis.
- It always gives the complete picture about the economy as whole hence it helps to understand working of the whole economy.
- Macro- economic has increased the utility of Ergonomics.
- It can be used for the development of micro- economic theories
- It helps in formulation of economic policies.

Limitations of MacroErgonomics (One-Liners):

- Aggregation Issues: Masks regional or income disparities.
- Oversimplified Models: Assumptions often ignore real-world complexities.
- Measurement Challenges: Inaccurate indicators (e.g., GDP, inflation).
- Microeconomic Ignorance: Overlooks individual and firm-level decisions.
- Unpredictability: Struggles with forecasting due to dynamic global factors.

- Policy Lag: Time delays reduce the effectiveness of fiscal and monetary policies.
- Markets and governments play complementary roles in Ergonomics to ensure efficient resource allocation, growth, and societal welfare.

Markets function as mechanisms for allocating resources through the forces of supply and demand. They determine prices, production levels, and distribution of goods and services based on consumer preferences and competition. Markets promote efficiency and innovation by encouraging competition among businesses. However, they may fail in cases of externalities (pollution), public goods (national defense), and monopolies.

Governments, on the other hand, step in to correct market failures, ensure fair competition, and provide public goods and services. They regulate markets, enforce property rights, and create policies to stabilize the economy through fiscal (taxing and spending) and monetary (money supply and interest rates) tools. Governments also promote equity through social programs and wealth redistribution, ensuring vulnerable populations are protected.

A balanced approach is essential: excessive reliance on markets may lead to inequality and market failures, while excessive government intervention can stifle innovation and efficiency. Ideally, markets drive economic activity, while governments create the framework for fair, sustainable, and stable economic growth.

Externalities refer to the unintended effects of an economic activity on third parties not directly involved in the activity. These effects can be beneficial (**positive externalities**) or harmful (**negative externalities**).

POSITIVE EXTERNALITIES

- Definition: Benefits enjoyed by third parties without paying for them.
- Examples:
  - Education: An educated workforce benefits society through higher productivity, innovation, and reduced crime rates.
  - Public Transportation: Reduces traffic congestion and pollution, benefiting everyone.
  - Research and Development (R&D): New technologies improve quality of life for society at large.
- Government Role: Positive externalities are often underprovided by the market, so governments may encourage them through subsidies, grants, or public provision.

NEGATIVE EXTERNALITIES

- Definition: Costs imposed on third parties without compensation.
- Examples:
  - Pollution: Factories emitting waste harm air and water quality for nearby residents.
  - Smoking: Secondhand smoke affects public health.
  - Deforestation: Leads to environmental damage and loss of biodiversity.
- Government Role: Negative externalities require intervention to internalize the costs, such as taxes (e.g., carbon tax), regulations, or penalties to discourage harmful activities.

For efficient resource allocation, policies aim to:

- Promote positive externalities (e.g., subsidies for education or healthcare).
- Mitigate negative externalities (e.g., environmental regulations or Pigouvian taxes). Addressing externalities ensures economic activities reflect their true social costs and benefits, improving overall welfare.

MODULE VII

CONSUMER AND PRODUCER BEHAVIOUR

Market – Demand and Supply – Determinants – Market equilibrium – elasticity of demand and supply – consumer behaviour – consumer equilibrium – Approaches to consumer behaviour – Production – Short-run and long-run Production Function – Returns to scale – economies Vs diseconomies of scale – Analysis of cost – Short-run and long-run cost function – Relation between Production and cost function.

Markets are platforms where consumers and producers interact to exchange goods and services. These interactions are governed by the forces of **demand** and **supply**, which together determine prices and the quantities traded in the market.

Demand represents consumer behavior, reflecting the quantity of a good or service that consumers are willing and able to purchase at various price levels. According to the law of demand, as the price of a product decreases, the quantity demanded typically increases, and vice versa. This inverse relationship is driven by factors such as consumer preferences, income levels, the price of related goods (substitutes and complements), and future expectations. For instance, a drop in Smartphone prices often leads to an increase in consumer demand.

Supply, on the other hand, reflects producer behavior and represents the quantity of a good or service that producers are willing and able to offer at different price levels. The law of supply states that as the price of a product increases, the quantity supplied also increases, due to higher potential profits. Producer behavior is influenced by production costs, advancements in technology, government policies, and market conditions. For example, higher coffee prices motivate farmers to grow and supply more coffee.

The interaction between demand and supply creates market equilibrium, where the quantity demanded equals the quantity supplied, resulting in a stable price. Consumers benefit from consumer surplus, which is the difference between what they are willing to pay and what they actually pay. Producers gain from producer surplus, which is the difference between their selling price and production costs. This dynamic balance ensures efficient allocation of resources in competitive markets.

DETERMINANTS OF DEMAND

Demand for a product or service is influenced by several factors:

1. Price of the Good: As price decreases, demand typically increases (law of demand).

2. Income of Consumers: Higher income increases demand for normal goods but decreases demand for inferior goods.

3. Prices of Related Goods:

- Substitutes: A rise in the price of one good increases demand for its substitute (e.g., tea and coffee).
- Complements: A rise in the price of one good decreases demand for its complement (e.g., cars and fuel).

4. Tastes and Preferences: Changes in consumer preferences directly affect demand.

5. Expectations of Future Prices: If consumers expect prices to rise, current demand increases.

6. Population Size: Larger populations tend to demand more goods and services.

Determinants of Supply

Supply is shaped by factors that influence producers' willingness and ability to sell:

1. Price of the Good: Higher prices incentivize more production (law of supply).
2. Cost of Production: Higher input costs (e.g., labor, materials) reduce supply.
3. Technology: Advancements lower production costs and increase supply.
4. Government Policies: Taxes and regulations reduce supply, while subsidies increase it.
5. Prices of Related Goods: A producer may shift resources to produce goods with higher profitability.
6. Number of Sellers: More sellers in the market increase supply.
7. Expectations of Future Prices: If producers expect higher prices, they may reduce current supply to sell later.

Market equilibrium occurs when the quantity demanded equals the quantity supplied at a specific price. At this point:

- There is no surplus (excess supply) or shortage (excess demand).
- The price at which equilibrium is achieved is called the equilibrium price, and the corresponding quantity is the equilibrium quantity.

If the market is not in equilibrium:

- Surplus: Occurs when supply exceeds demand at a given price, causing downward pressure on prices.
- Shortage: Occurs when demand exceeds supply, leading to upward pressure on prices.

Equilibrium can shift due to changes in demand or supply determinants. For instance, an increase in consumer income (a determinant of demand) may lead to higher equilibrium prices and quantities, while advancements in technology (a determinant of supply) may lower equilibrium prices and increase output.

Efficient markets adjust dynamically; ensuring resources are allocated where they are most valued. Understanding these determinants helps predict changes in prices and quantities, crucial for both businesses and policymakers.

Elasticity refers to the responsiveness of quantity demanded or supplied to a change in price or other factors. It measures how sensitive consumers and producers are to price changes.

Elasticity of Demand

- Definition: The elasticity of demand measures how the quantity demanded of a good changes in response to a change in its price. It is often referred to as price elasticity of demand (PED).

- Formula:

$$PED = \frac{\% \text{ change in quantity demanded}}{\% \text{ change in price}}$$

Types of Elasticity:

1. Elastic Demand (PED > 1): Demand is highly responsive to price changes. A small price change leads to a larger percentage change in quantity demanded.
    - Example: Luxury goods, non-essential items.

2. **Inelastic Demand (PED < 1):** Demand is less responsive to price changes. A price change results in a smaller percentage change in quantity demanded.
   - Example: Necessities like insulin, basic utilities.
3. **Unitary Elastic Demand (PED = 1):** A price change results in a proportional change in quantity demanded.
4. **Perfectly Elastic Demand (PED = ∞):** Consumers will only buy at one price and will stop buying if the price increases even slightly.
   - Example: Commodities with perfect substitutes.
5. **Perfectly Inelastic Demand (PED = 0):** Quantity demanded does not change regardless of price changes.
   - Example: Life-saving medication with no substitutes. **Elasticity of Supply**

- Definition: The elasticity of supply measures how the quantity supplied of a good changes in response to a change in its price. It is called price elasticity of supply (PES).

- Formula:

$$PES = \frac{\% \text{ change in quantity supplied}}{\% \text{ change in price}}$$

Types of Elasticity:

1. **Elastic Supply (PES > 1):** Supply is highly responsive to price changes. A small price change leads to a larger percentage change in quantity supplied.

- Example: Manufactured goods with flexible production processes.

2. Inelastic Supply (PES < 1): Supply is less responsive to price changes. A price change results in a smaller percentage change in quantity supplied.

    - Example: Goods that require a long production time, such as artwork or land.

3. Unitary Elastic Supply (PES = 1): A price change results in a proportional change in quantity supplied.

4. Perfectly Elastic Supply (PES = ∞): Producers are willing to supply any quantity at a specific price, but none at a higher or lower price.

5. Perfectly Inelastic Supply (PES = 0): Quantity supplied does not change regardless of price changes.

    - Example: Unique products like rare artifacts.

CONSUMER BEHAVIOUR

Consumer behavior studies how individuals make decisions to allocate their limited resources (income) to purchase goods and services to maximize satisfaction (utility). It is influenced by:

1. Preferences and Tastes: Consumers choose goods based on their personal preferences.
2. Income: Determines purchasing power and the ability to buy goods.
3. Prices of Goods: Higher prices reduce the quantity demanded, and lower prices increase it (law of demand).

4. Substitutes and Complements: The availability and prices of related goods affect choices.
5. Expectations: Anticipation of future prices, income changes, or product availability impacts decisions.

Consumers aim to maximize their utility by allocating resources in a way that provides the most satisfaction while staying within their budget constraints.

CONSUMER EQUILIBRIUM

Consumer equilibrium occurs when a consumer allocates their income in such a way that maximizes their total utility, given their budget constraint and the prices of goods.

Conditions for Consumer Equilibrium

1. For a Single Good: The consumer is in equilibrium when the marginal utility per unit of currency spent (MU/P) equals the price of the good:

    Marginal Utility (MU)=Price (P)

2. For Multiple Goods: The consumer equilibrium condition is satisfied when the marginal utility per unit of currency spent is equalized across all goods:

    $$\frac{MU_x}{P_x} = \frac{MU_y}{P_y}$$

    Where:
    - MU_x and MU_y are the marginal utilities of goods X and Y.
    - P_x and P_y are their respective prices.

Key Concepts:

- Budget Constraint: The consumer cannot spend more than their total income.
- Indifference Curve Analysis: In graphical terms, equilibrium is where the consumer's budget line is tangent to the indifference curve (representing equal utility levels). At this point, the consumer achieves maximum utility within their budget.

Significance of Consumer Equilibrium •

- Explains how consumers make optimal choices given limited resources.
- Helps businesses understand consumer preferences to set prices and promote goods effectively.
- Assists policymakers in analyzing how changes in taxes, subsidies, or income levels affect consumer welfare.

There are two main approaches to understanding **consumer equilibrium**: the **Cardinal Utility Approach** and the **Ordinal Utility Approach**. Both explain how consumers allocate their income to maximize satisfaction but differ in their assumptions and methods.

1. Cardinal Utility Approach

This approach assumes that utility (satisfaction) can be measured quantitatively in cardinal terms, such as in "utils."

Conditions for Consumer Equilibrium:

- Single Good: A consumer is in equilibrium when the marginal utility (MU) of the good equals its price:

$MU = P$

- Multiple Goods: When multiple goods are consumed, equilibrium is achieved when the marginal utility per unit of currency spent is equal for all goods:

$$\frac{MU_x}{P_x} = \frac{MU_y}{P_y} = \ldots = \frac{MU_n}{P_n}$$

Where:

- MU_x, MU_y: Marginal utilities of goods X and Y.
- P_x, P_y: Prices of goods X and Y.

Limitations:

- Utility is subjective and cannot be measured accurately in cardinal terms.
- Assumes constant marginal utility of money, which may not be realistic.

2. Ordinal Utility Approach (Indifference Curve Analysis)

This approach assumes that utility cannot be measured numerically but can be ranked or ordered. It uses indifference curves and budget constraints to determine consumer equilibrium.

Key Concepts:

- Indifference Curve (IC): Represents combinations of two goods that provide the same level of satisfaction.
- Budget Line: Represents all possible combinations of two goods that the consumer can afford given their income and prices.

Conditions for Consumer Equilibrium:

- The consumer is in equilibrium where the budget line is tangent to the highest possible indifference curve. At this point:

Where:

- MRS: Marginal Rate of Substitution (rate at which a consumer is willing to substitute one good for another while maintaining the same level of satisfaction).
- $\frac{P_x}{P_y}$: Price ratio of goods X and Y.

$$MRS = \frac{P_x}{P_y}$$

Advantages:

- More realistic, as it avoids measuring utility in absolute terms. ☐ Captures consumer preferences and trade-offs.

PRODUCTION

Production refers to the process of combining inputs like labor, capital, land, and raw materials to create goods and services that satisfy human wants. It is a key economic activity and forms the basis of supply in markets.

Types of Production:

1. Primary Production: Involves extracting natural resources, such as farming, fishing, and mining.
2. Secondary Production: Involves manufacturing and industrial processes that transform raw materials into finished goods.
3. Tertiary Production: Includes services like retail, education, and healthcare that support consumers and businesses.

Factors of Production:

- Land: Natural resources used in production.
- Labor: Human effort, both physical and mental, involved in production.
- Capital: Machinery, tools, and buildings used to produce goods and services.
- Entrepreneurship: The ability to organize resources, take risks, and innovate.

Importance of Production:

- Satisfies human wants by creating goods and services.
- Drives economic growth and increases national income.
- Creates employment opportunities.
- Enhances standard of living by improving resource utilization.

Production efficiency, achieved by minimizing costs and maximizing output, ensures that resources are used effectively to meet market demand.

PRODUCTION FUNCTIONS

The production function relates the quantity of factor inputs used by a business to the amount of output that result.

We use three measures of production and productivity:

- Total product (total output). In manufacturing industries such as motor vehicles, it is straightforward to measure how much output is being produced. In service or knowledge industries, where output is less "tangible" it is harder to measure productivity.

- Average product measures output per-worker-employed or output-per-unit of capital.
- Marginal product is the change in output from increasing the number of workers used by one person, or by adding one more machine to the production process *in the short run*.

SHORT RUN PRODUCTION FUNCTION

- The short run is a time period where at least one factor of production is in fixed supply. A business has chosen its scale of production and sticks with this in the short run.
- We assume that the quantity of plant and machinery is fixed and that production can be altered by changing variable inputs such as labour, raw materials and energy.

Diminishing Returns

The key concept of short-run production is the Law of Diminishing Marginal Returns. It states that as more units of a variable input (e.g., labor) are added to a fixed input (e.g., capital or land), the additional output (marginal product) from each extra unit of the variable input eventually decreases.

Initially, adding more workers or resources can lead to increased productivity due to better utilization of fixed inputs. However, as the variable input continues to increase, inefficiencies arise, such as overcrowding or limited machinery, causing the marginal product to decline.

For example, in a factory with a fixed number of machines, hiring more workers may initially boost output as machines are used more effectively. Eventually, with too many workers and the same number of machines, each additional worker contributes less to production because the machines become over utilized.

This concept helps businesses understand the limits of increasing production in the short run and highlights the importance of balancing inputs for optimal efficiency. It also explains why short-run costs rise as output increases, as diminishing returns cause marginal costs to escalate.

LONG RUN PRODUCTION FUNCTION

The long run is a period during which all inputs, including capital, are variable. Firms can change the scale of production by adjusting all factors of production.

The long-run production function differs fundamentally from its short-run counterpart by allowing complete flexibility in input adjustments. This flexibility provides businesses the opportunity to optimize production processes fully.

Key Aspects of the Long-Run Production Function

- Total Input Variability: Unlike the short-run, where certain inputs remain fixed, the longrun scenario allows firms to vary all inputs, including labour, capital, and technology.
- Time Horizon: The long-run is not defined by a specific time frame but is characterised as the period where all inputs can be varied, allowing for complete adjustment in production capacity.
- Strategic Decision-Making: In the long run, firms can make strategic decisions like changing production techniques, scaling operations, or introducing new technologies.

Returns to Scale: Expanding Output

Returns to scale in the long-run production function play a pivotal role in determining how output changes with a proportional change in all inputs. These returns are categorised based on the ratio of output change to input change.

Types of Returns to Scale

1. Increasing Returns to Scale (IRS): Characterised by a more than proportional increase in output relative to inputs. This often results from efficiencies in mass production or enhanced managerial effectiveness.
2. Constant Returns to Scale (CRS): When output increases in direct proportion to inputs, indicating a stable and predictable expansion path for the firm.
3. Decreasing Returns to Scale (DRS): Occurs when the output increases by a smaller proportion than inputs, often due to inefficiencies and complexities associated with large-scale operations.

ECONOMIES OF SCALE

Economies of scale refer to the cost advantages that a firm experiences as it increases production. As the scale of production grows, the average cost per unit of output decreases due to better utilization of resources.

Types of Economies of Scale:

1. Internal Economies of Scale: Cost savings within the firm.
    - Technical: Efficient use of machinery or advanced technology.

- Managerial: Specialized management improves efficiency.
- Financial: Larger firms access credit at lower interest rates.
- Marketing: Bulk buying or advertising reduces per-unit costs.
- Risk-Bearing: Diversifying products reduces risks.

2. External Economies of Scale: Cost savings due to industry-wide growth.
    - Improved infrastructure, skilled labor availability, or supplier networks.

Benefits:

- Lower costs per unit.
- Competitive pricing.
- Increased profitability.

DISECONOMIES OF SCALE

Diseconomies of scale occur when a firm's expansion leads to higher average costs per unit. This typically happens when inefficiencies arise at very large scales of production.

Causes of Diseconomies of Scale:

1. Internal Diseconomies: Inefficiencies within the firm.
    - Managerial: Difficulty in coordination and communication. o Overcrowding: Reduced employee productivity due to supervision challenges.

- Resource Limitations: Scarcity of raw materials increases costs.

2. External Diseconomies: Costs rise due to industry growth.

    - Increased competition for resources or infrastructure overload.

Implications:

- Higher costs per unit.
- Reduced profitability.
- Loss of competitive advantage.

Economies of Scale: Cost per unit decreases as production increases.

Diseconomies of Scale: Cost per unit increases when production becomes too large.

Efficient scaling requires firms to find the balance between achieving economies and avoiding diseconomies of scale.

COST ANALYSIS

Cost analysis refers to the process of examining and evaluating the financial implications of various business decisions, projects, or initiatives. It involves identifying, measuring, and comparing the costs and benefits associated with different options to determine the most cost effective and efficient solution. For data teams, cost analysis is crucial as it helps assess expenses related to data infrastructure, tools, personnel, and other resources, and evaluate the return on investment (ROI) generated by the team's activities. This enables data teams to make informed decisions about resource allocation, prioritize projects, and optimize their operations to maximize value while minimizing costs.

- Resource allocation: Cost analysis helps data teams allocate resources efficiently to maximize ROI.
- Project prioritization: By understanding the costs and benefits of different projects, data teams can prioritize initiatives that offer the highest value.
- Operational optimization: Cost analysis enables data teams to identify areas for improvement and optimize their operations to reduce costs and increase efficiency.

SHORT-RUN COST FUNCTION

The short-run cost function represents the relationship between output and the various costs a firm incurs in the short run, where at least one input (e.g., capital) is fixed.

Components of Short-Run Costs

1. Total Fixed Cost (TFC):
    - Costs that remain constant regardless of the level of output.
    - Example: Rent, salaries of permanent staff. ⬜ TFC = Constant
2. Total Variable Cost (TVC):
    - Costs that vary with the level of output, such as raw materials and wages of hourly workers.
    - TVC = f(Q)
    - Q = quantity of output
3. Total Cost (TC):
    - The sum of fixed and variable costs:
    - TC = TFC + TVC

Per-Unit (Average) Costs

1. Average Fixed Cost (AFC): Fixed cost per unit of output, which decreases as output increases:

   $AFC = TFC/Q$

2. Average Variable Cost (AVC): Variable cost per unit of output:

   $AVC = TVC/Q$

3. Average Total Cost (ATC): Total cost per unit of output:

   $ATC = TC/Q = AFC + AVC$

Marginal Cost (MC)

Marginal cost is the additional cost incurred to produce one more unit of output:

$MC = dTC/dQ$

Cost Behavior in the Short Run

- AFC continuously decreases as output increases because fixed costs are spread over more units.
- AVC and ATC initially decrease due to efficiency but later increase as the law of diminishing marginal returns sets in.
- MC decreases initially but rises after a certain point, intersecting AVC and ATC at their minimum points.

LONG-RUN COST FUNCTION

The long-run cost function represents the relationship between the output (QQQ) and the cost incurred when all inputs are variable, meaning there are no fixed costs. In the long run, a firm can adjust all factors of production (e.g., labor, capital, land) to achieve the most cost-efficient production level.

Key Features of the Long-Run Cost Function

1. No Fixed Costs: All costs are variable because firms have the flexibility to adjust inputs. TC = TVC
2. Economies of Scale: As production increases, average costs (ACACAC) decrease due to efficiency gains from larger-scale operations.
3. Diseconomies of Scale: After reaching an optimal production level, further increases in output may lead to higher average costs due to inefficiencies.
4. Long-Run Average Cost Curve (LRAC): The LRAC curve is derived from the short-run cost curves and represents the lowest cost of production at each level of output when all inputs can be adjusted. It is typically U-shaped, reflecting economies and diseconomies of scale.

Components in Long Run Cost

1. Total Cost (TC):

    In the long run, TC depends on the combination of inputs that minimizes cost for a given output:

    $TC = f(Q)$

2. Average Cost (AC) : $AC = TC/Q$

3. Marginal Cost (MC): $MC = dTC/dq$

    - The LRAC curve is an envelope curve that envelopes all possible short-run average cost curves.
    - Firms adjust their scale of operations in the long run to operate at the most efficient output level, typically at the minimum point of the LRAC curve.

The long-run cost function is crucial for strategic planning, such as deciding plant size, production technology, and market pricing strategies.

RELATION BETWEEN PRODUCTION FUNCTION AND COST FUNCTION

The production function and cost function are closely related in Ergonomics, as they describe two sides of the production process. The production function focuses on the output generated from inputs, while the cost function relates to the cost incurred to produce that output. The link between the two arises because the level of inputs required for production directly determines the cost.

Key Relationships

1. **Inputs and Costs:**

   - The production function describes the relationship between inputs (e.g., labor, capital) and output (QQQ).
   - The cost function is derived from the production function, as inputs have prices. For example:

$$TC = \sum (\text{Input Quantity} \times \text{Input Price})$$

2. **Marginal Relationships:**

   - The Marginal Product (MP) of an input (e.g., labor) indicates the additional output from using one more unit of the input.
   - The Marginal Cost (MC) reflects the additional cost of producing one more unit of output.

   There is an inverse relationship between marginal product and marginal cost:

$$MC = \frac{\text{Input Price}}{MP}$$

3. **Diminishing Marginal Returns and Increasing Costs:**

    - In the short run, the law of diminishing marginal returns states that as more of a variable input (e.g., labor) is added to a fixed input (e.g., capital), the marginal product eventually decreases.
    - This leads to rising marginal costs, as more input is needed to produce additional output.

4. **Returns to Scale and Long-Run Costs:**

    - In the long run, the production function reflects returns to scale (increasing, constant, or decreasing).
    - Increasing returns to scale lead to economies of scale (lower average costs), while decreasing returns to scale cause diseconomies of scale (higher average costs).

The production function determines how efficiently inputs are converted into output, while the cost function quantifies the expenses of using those inputs. A firm's goal is to optimize production to minimize costs and maximize profits, making the relationship between these two functions fundamental to managerial decision-making.

MODULE VIII

PRODUCT AND FACTOR MARKET

Product market – perfect and imperfect market – different market structures – Firm's equilibrium and supply – Market efficiency – Economic costs of imperfect competition – factor market – Land, Labour and capital – Demand and supply – determination of factor price – Interaction of product and factor market – General equilibrium and efficiency of competitive markets.

A **product market** is a platform where goods and services are bought and sold. In the context of managerial Ergonomics, it refers to the interaction between firms (producers) and consumers where firms supply products, and consumers create demand. The product market plays a critical role in determining prices, output levels, and profitability.

Key Features:

1. Supply and Demand Interaction:
    - Firms supply goods/services based on production costs and profit goals.
    - Consumers demand goods/services based on preferences, incomes, and prices.

2. Market Structures:
    - Product markets can operate under various market structures, such as:
        - Perfect Competition: Many sellers, identical products.
        - Monopoly: Single seller, unique product.
        - Monopolistic Competition: Many sellers, differentiated products.

- Oligopoly: Few sellers, interdependent pricing.
3. Price Determination:
   a. Prices are determined by the equilibrium between supply and demand, influenced by production costs, consumer preferences, and competition.
4. Role in Decision-Making:
   a) Managerial Ergonomics uses the product market analysis to make decisions about pricing, output, advertising, and market entry strategies.

The product market is a vital area of focus for firms to align production and marketing strategies with consumer preferences and market competition. By analyzing demand-supply interactions, cost structures, and market trends, managerial Ergonomics helps businesses make informed decisions to maximize profits and efficiency.

Perfect markets represent an ideal scenario of efficiency, while **imperfect markets** reflect realworld conditions where firms influence prices and competition varies. Managerial decisions in imperfect markets require strategies like differentiation and innovation to thrive.

Perfect Market

A perfect market is an idealized market structure where all firms and consumers operate under certain conditions that ensure maximum efficiency.

Key characteristics include:

1. Large Number of Buyers and Sellers: No single buyer or seller can influence the market price.
2. Homogeneous Products: All goods are identical, with no differentiation.

3. Free Entry and Exit: Firms can easily enter or exit the market without barriers.
4. Perfect Information: All participants have complete knowledge of prices and products.
5. Price Takers: Firms accept the market price determined by supply and demand.

Example: Agricultural markets like wheat or rice often approximate perfect markets.

Imperfect Market

An imperfect market deviates from the conditions of a perfect market, leading to inefficiencies. Characteristics include:

1. Fewer Buyers or Sellers: Some firms or buyers may influence prices (e.g., monopolies or oligopolies).
2. Product Differentiation: Goods are not identical, and firms compete through quality, branding, or features.
3. Barriers to Entry: High costs or legal restrictions prevent new firms from entering easily.
4. Incomplete Information: Buyers or sellers may lack full knowledge about prices or products.
5. Price Makers: Firms can influence or set prices in certain cases.

Examples: Monopoly (e.g., utilities), monopolistic competition (e.g., retail clothing), or oligopoly (e.g., the automobile industry).

MARKET STRUCTURES

Market structures refer to the organizational and competitive characteristics of a market that influence the behavior of firms and their pricing and output decisions. It is a key concept in Ergonomics and managerial decision-making.

Types of Market Structures

Market structures are categorized based on the number of sellers, product characteristics, barriers to entry, and pricing power. The four main types are:

1. **Perfect Competition**
   - Characteristics:
     - Large number of buyers and sellers.
     - Homogeneous (identical) products. o   Free entry and exit of firms. o   Perfect knowledge of prices and products.
     - Firms are price takers (cannot influence market price).
   - Examples: Agricultural markets like wheat, rice, or corn.
   - Key Insights:
     - Prices are determined by market supply and demand.
     - Maximum efficiency is achieved, with optimal resource allocation.

2. **Monopoly**
   - Characteristics:
     - Single seller controls the market. o   No close substitutes for the product. o   Significant barriers to entry (e.g., legal, natural, or technological).
     - The firm is a price maker (sets prices by controlling supply).
   - Examples: Utility companies (electricity, water supply).
   - Key Insights:
     - May result in higher prices and lower output.
     - Often regulated to prevent abuse of market power.

3. **Monopolistic Competition**

    - Characteristics:
        - Many sellers offering differentiated products (e.g., branding, quality).
        - Some control over pricing due to differentiation.
        - Relatively easy entry and exit.
    - Examples: Restaurants, clothing brands, consumer electronics.
    - Key Insights:
        - Encourages innovation and variety. o May result in inefficiencies like higher costs and prices due to advertising and differentiation efforts.

4. **Oligopoly**

    - Characteristics:
        - A few large firms dominate the market.
        - Interdependence among firms (actions of one firm affect others). o Products may be homogeneous (e.g., steel) or differentiated (e.g., automobiles).
        - Significant barriers to entry (e.g., high capital requirements).
    - Examples: Automobile manufacturers, airline industry, telecom providers.
    - Key Insights:
        - Firms may engage in collusion or price wars.
        - Competition may focus on non-price factors like innovation or advertising.

Other Types (Less Common)

a. Duopoly: A special case of oligopoly with only two dominant firms (e.g., Airbus and Boeing).
b. Monopsony: A market with a single buyer (e.g., government procurement markets).
c. Oligopsony: A market with few buyers but many sellers (e.g., agricultural commodities).

FIRM'S EQUILIBRIUM AND SUPPLY

In Ergonomics, a firm's equilibrium refers to the point where a firm maximizes its profit or minimizes its loss. It occurs when the firm's revenue and costs are balanced in such a way that the firm has no incentive to alter its production level. The concept of equilibrium is closely tied to the firm's supply behavior, as the supply of a product is directly influenced by the firm's production decisions.

Firm's Equilibrium

Definition: A firm is in equilibrium when it achieves maximum profit (or minimizes losses) given its cost structure and market conditions. This is determined by the relationship between marginal revenue (MR) and marginal cost (MC).

1. **Conditions for Equilibrium:**
    - Profit Maximization Rule: MR=MC, At this point, the additional revenue from selling one more unit equals the additional cost of producing it.
    - No Incentive to Change Output:

   At equilibrium, the firm neither increases nor decreases its output as any deviation would lead to lower profits or higher losses.

2. **Short-Run vs. Long-Run Equilibrium:**
   - In the short run, a firm can operate with fixed factors of production, and it may earn profits, break even, or incur losses.
   - In the long run, all inputs are variable, and firms adjust their production scale. Firms may enter or exit the market, and equilibrium occurs when firms earn only normal profit (zero economic profit).

Supply and Firm's Behaviour

1. **Supply Curve:**
   - The supply curve shows the relationship between the price of a good and the quantity a firm is willing to supply.
   - It is derived from the firm's marginal cost curve in the short run because a firm supplies output where $P = MC$.

2. **Law of Supply:**
   - As the price of a product increases, firms are willing to supply more because higher prices improve profitability.
   - Conversely, at lower prices, the quantity supplied decreases.

3. **Short-Run Supply:**
   - In the short run, supply depends on variable factors of production and the firm's ability to cover variable costs.
   - If the market price falls below the average variable cost (AVC), the firm will shut down production.

4. **Long-Run Supply:**
   - In the long run, firms can adjust all inputs and enter or exit the market.

- Supply is determined by the point where firms earn normal profit, ensuring sustainable production.

5. **Market Supply Curve:**
    - The market supply curve is the horizontal summation of the supply curves of all individual firms in the market.

MARKET EFFICIENCY

Market efficiency refers to the extent to which markets allocate resources optimally, ensuring that goods and services are produced, distributed, and consumed in a manner that maximizes societal welfare. It occurs when prices in a market fully reflect all available information, and resources are allocated to their most valuable uses without waste or misallocation.

Types of Market Efficiency

1. **Allocative Efficiency**
    - Occurs when resources are distributed in a way that maximizes consumer and producer surplus.
    - Goods and services are produced in quantities that match consumer preferences,

        i.e., where P = MC (price equals marginal cost).

2. **Productive Efficiency:**
    - Achieved when firms produce goods at the lowest possible cost.
    - This happens at the minimum point of the average total cost (ATC) curve.

3. **Dynamic Efficiency:**
    - Relates to innovation and technological progress over time.

- Markets are dynamically efficient when they foster investment in research and development, leading to better products and processes.

4. **Informational Efficiency:**

    - Exists when market prices reflect all available information.
    - Associated with the Efficient Market Hypothesis (EMH) in financial markets.

Conditions for Market Efficiency

1. Perfect Competition: Many buyers and sellers ensure no single entity influences prices.
2. Perfect Information: All market participants have access to accurate and complete information.
3. No Externalities: External costs or benefits (e.g., pollution) are absent or internalized.
4. Free Entry and Exit: Firms can enter or exit the market without barriers.

ECONOMIC COST OF IMPERFECT COMPETITION

Imperfect competition refers to market structures where firms have some degree of control over prices and output, deviating from the conditions of perfect competition. While these structures (e.g., monopoly, monopolistic competition, and oligopoly) exist in most real-world markets, they come with significant economic costs that impact resource allocation, consumer welfare, and overall efficiency.

Key Economic Costs of Imperfect Competition

1. **Allocative Inefficiency:**

    - In imperfect competition, firms often produce less and charge higher prices than in perfect competition.
    - This results in a deadweight loss—a loss of total surplus (consumer and producer surplus) because not all mutually beneficial trades take place.
    - Allocative inefficiency occurs because P>MCP > MCP>MC, meaning resources are not distributed in a way that maximizes societal welfare.

2. **Productive Inefficiency:**

    - Firms in imperfectly competitive markets may not produce at the lowest average total cost (ATC), especially in monopolistic competition, where firms operate with excess capacity.
    - This leads to higher costs per unit and inefficient use of resources.

3. **Reduced Consumer Surplus:**

    - Higher prices charged by firms reduce consumer surplus (the difference between what consumers are willing to pay and what they actually pay).
    - Consumers often pay more for less variety and lower quality compared to perfectly competitive markets.

4. **Barriers to Entry and Market Power:**
   - In monopolies or oligopolies, barriers to entry (e.g., patents, economies of scale, and regulatory constraints) limit competition.
   - This restricts innovation and prevents new entrants from offering better or cheaper alternatives to consumers.

5. **Limited Innovation:**
   - While monopolies may invest in research and development (due to their financial resources), they also have less incentive to innovate since they face little to no competition.
   - Oligopolies may focus on non-price competition (e.g., advertising) instead of improving products or production methods.

6. **Advertising and Branding Costs:**
   - Firms in monopolistic competition and oligopoly spend heavily on advertising to differentiate their products, leading to higher costs that are ultimately passed on to consumers.
   - These expenses do not necessarily contribute to improved product quality or societal welfare.

7. **Market Distortions from Collusion:**
   - In oligopolies, firms may engage in collusion (formal or tacit agreements to fix prices or limit production), further reducing output and increasing prices.
   - Collusive practices lead to artificial scarcity and harm consumer welfare.

8. **Social Inequality:**
    - Imperfect competition often leads to wealth concentration, as firms with significant market power earn substantial profits, benefiting owners and shareholders disproportionately.
    - This exacerbates income and wealth inequality in the economy.

Examples of Economic Costs

- Monopoly: A utility company charging excessively high prices for electricity due to the lack of competition.
- Oligopoly: Collusion among airlines to raise ticket prices, reducing consumer choice and welfare.
- Monopolistic Competition: Overuse of advertising in the fast-food industry, leading to higher costs without substantial improvement in product quality.

FACTOR MARKET

The factor market refers to the marketplace where factors of production—land, labor, capital, and entrepreneurship—are bought and sold. It is essential for the functioning of an economy as it facilitates the allocation of resources required for the production of goods and services.

Key Features:

1. **Participants:**
    - Firms: Act as buyers, demanding factors of production to produce goods and services.

- Households: Act as sellers, providing factors like labor, land, or capital in exchange for income (wages, rent, interest, profit).

2. **Types of Factor Markets:**
    - Labor Market: Where labor services are exchanged for wages.
    - Capital Market: Where financial resources like loans and investments are allocated.
    - Land Market: Where land is leased or sold for production purposes.

3. **Price Determination:**
    - Prices of factors (wages for labor, rent for land, interest for capital) are determined by the interaction of demand and supply in the factor market.

4. **Derived Demand:**
    - The demand for factors of production is derived from the demand for the final goods and services they help produce.

Importance:

- Ensures efficient allocation of resources.
- Influences income distribution in the economy.
- Plays a critical role in determining production costs and profitability.

LAND, LABOR, AND CAPITAL

Land, labor, and capital are three primary factors of production essential for producing goods and services. These inputs, along with entrepreneurship, drive economic activity and are fundamental to resource allocation and income distribution.

1. Land

- Definition: Land refers to all natural resources used in production, such as soil, minerals, forests, water, and climate.
- Characteristics:
    - Fixed Supply: The total amount of land is limited.
    - Immobility: Land cannot be moved from one location to another.
    - Heterogeneity: The quality of land varies by region.
- Return: The income earned from land is called rent.
- Importance: Land is crucial for agriculture, mining, real estate, and other resource-based industries.

2. Labor

- Definition: Labor represents human effort (physical and mental) used in the production process.
- Characteristics:
    - Human Element: Labor is performed by individuals with skills, abilities, and preferences.
    - Inseparability: Labor cannot be separated from the worker.

- Perishable: Labor is lost if not utilized, as time cannot be stored.
- Skill Variance: Labor differs in skill levels, from unskilled to highly skilled workers.

- Return: The income earned by labor is called wages or salaries.
- Importance: Labor drives productivity, innovation, and the creation of goods and services.

3. Capital

- Definition: Capital refers to man-made resources used to produce goods and services, such as machinery, tools, buildings, and equipment.
- Characteristics:
    - Man-Made: Unlike land, capital is created by human effort.
    - Durability: Capital goods have a lifespan and are used repeatedly.
    - Enhances Productivity: Capital increases the efficiency of labor and land.
- Types of Capital:
    - Physical Capital: Machinery, tools, and infrastructure.
    - Financial Capital: Money used for investment.
    - Human Capital: Skills and knowledge of the workforce.
- Return: The income earned from capital is called interest or profit.

- Importance: Capital investment boosts productivity and economic growth.

DEMAND AND SUPPLY

Demand

- Definition: Demand refers to the quantity of a good or service that consumers are willing and able to purchase at various prices, during a given period of time.

- Law of Demand: There is an inverse relationship between price and quantity demanded. As the price of a goods increases, the quantity demanded decreases, and vice versa (ceteris paribus).

Determinants of Demand:

- Price: Higher prices typically reduce demand.

- Income: As consumer income rises, demand for normal goods increases.

- Tastes and Preferences: Changes in consumer preferences can shift demand.

- Substitute Goods: If the price of a substitute rises, demand for the good may increase.

- Complementary Goods: If the price of a complement rises, demand for the good may decrease

- Expectations: If consumers expect prices to rise in the future, they may increase current demand.

- Population: A larger population increases demand for goods and services.

- Demand Curve: A graph that shows the relationship between the price of a good and the quantity demanded. It typically slopes downward from left to right.

Supply

- Definition: Supply refers to the quantity of a good or service that producers are willing and able to produce and sell at various prices, during a given period of time.

- Law of Supply: There is a direct relationship between price and quantity supplied. As the price of a goods increases, the quantity supplied increases, and vice versa (ceteris paribus).

Determinants of Supply:

- Price: Higher prices provide an incentive for producers to supply more.

- Production Costs: If the cost of production rises (e.g., due to higher wages or raw material costs), supply decreases.

- Technology: Technological advancements can increase supply by making production more efficient.

- Number of Sellers: More firms in the market generally increase supply.

- Expectations: If producers expect higher prices in the future, they may reduce current supply to sell at higher prices later.

- Government Policies: Taxes, subsidies, and regulations can affect supply.
- Supply Curve: A graph showing the relationship between the price of a good and the quantity supplied. It typically slopes upward from left to right.

DETERMINATION OF FACTOR PRICES

The price of a factor of production—such as labor, land, or capital—is determined in the factor markets, where these factors are bought and sold. Factor prices are influenced by the interaction of supply and demand for each factor of production. Here's an explanation of how factor prices are determined:

Labor (Wages)

- **Demand for Labor**
    - The demand for labor is derived from the demand for the goods and services that labor helps produce. Firms will demand more labor when the marginal revenue product (MRP) of labor is high. The MRP is the additional revenue generated by employing an additional unit of labor.
    - The law of diminishing returns states that as more labor is added, the additional output (marginal product) from each additional worker will eventually decline. Hence, the demand for labor will eventually decrease as the wage rate rises, given a fixed amount of capital and technology.
- **Supply of Labor:**
    - The supply of labor depends on the number of workers available and their willingness to work at different wage

levels. Factors such as population size, education, migration, and worker preferences influence the labor supply.

- As wages increase, the supply of labor increases, but the relationship may also depend on factors like work-life balance, job conditions, and alternative employment opportunities.

- **Equilibrium Wage:**
    - The equilibrium wage rate is determined at the point where the demand for labor equals the supply of labor. At this wage rate, the quantity of labor that firms wish to hire equals the quantity of labor that workers are willing to supply.
    2.Land (Rent) ☐ Demand for Land:
    - The demand for land is driven by its use in producing goods and services (e.g., agriculture, real estate, minning). The more productive or valuable land is for production, the higher its demand.
    - The rent paid for land is based on its productivity and location. More fertile agricultural land or land in prime locations for business will demand higher rents. ☐ Supply of Land:
    - The supply of land is fixed in the short run (since land is a finite resource). In the long run, however, factors such as land reclamation, land development, or policy changes (e.g., land use zoning) can influence the effective supply of land.

- **Equilibrium Rent:**
    - The price of land (rent) is determined by the equilibrium between the demand for land (driven by its

productivity and use) and the supply (which is limited by geography and availability).

Capital (Interest)

- **Demand for Capital:**
    - The demand for capital comes from businesses needing tools, machinery, buildings, and other equipment to produce goods and services. The demand for capital depends on the marginal productivity of capital (MPC)—the additional output generated by an additional unit of capital.
    - As businesses increase production, they require more capital, and thus the demand for capital increases.

- **Supply of Capital:**
    - The supply of capital comes from savings and investments. Individuals, firms, and governments provide funds to financial markets where capital is loaned out to borrowers. The availability of capital is influenced by interest rates, savings behavior, and government policies (e.g., fiscal or monetary policy).

- **Equilibrium Interest Rate:**
    - The interest rate (the price of capital) is determined by the balance of demand and supply for capital. When the demand for capital increases (e.g., businesses want to invest more), the interest rate tends to rise, and when the supply of capital increases (e.g., more savings are available for lending), the interest rate tends to fall.

Entrepreneurship (Profit)

- **Demand for Entrepreneurship:**
    - Entrepreneurs are required to organize and combine the factors of production to create goods and services. The demand for entrepreneurship is driven by business opportunities, market demand, and the potential for innovation and profit.

- **Supply of Entrepreneurship:**
    - The supply of entrepreneurs is influenced by factors such as risk tolerance, access to capital, and government policies that encourage or discourage entrepreneurship.

- **Equilibrium Profit:**
    - Profits are determined by the overall success of business ventures. The equilibrium profit rate is the return earned by entrepreneurs for taking the risks associated with organizing and combining resources. It is influenced by competition, technological advances, and market demand.

INTERACTION OF PRODUCT MARKET AND FACTOR MARKET

The product market and the factor market are two interconnected components of an economy that work together to drive production, income generation, and the distribution of goods and services. These markets interact continuously, influencing one another and contributing to the overall functioning of the economy.

1. **Demand-Supply Link:** Firms in the factor market demand labor, capital, and land to produce goods. The output produced in the product market depends on the availability and price of these factors. For example, a higher demand for a product in the product market can lead to an increased demand for labor in the factor market.

2. **Revenue and Cost:** The revenue that firms generate from selling goods in the product market is used to pay for the factors of production in the factor market. For example, wages are paid to laborers, rent is paid for land, and interest is paid for capital.

3. **Circular Flow:** There is a circular flow of income between the two markets. Firms receive income from the product market, which is used to compensate the factors of production (labor, capital, land) in the factor market. These factors, in turn, provide income to households, then spent on products in the product market.

4. **Influence of Prices:** Changes in factor prices can affect the cost structure of firms, which may impact the prices and supply of goods in the product market. Conversely, shifts in demand for goods in the product market can influence firms' demand for factors of production.

GENERAL EQUILIBRIUM AND EFFICIENCY OF COMPETITIVE MARKETS

General equilibrium refers to a situation in an economy where all markets (for goods, services, and factors of production) are simultaneously in equilibrium, meaning that supply equals demand in each market. In this state, every individual or firm makes decisions that are in balance with others, and there are no tendencies for prices or quantities to change.

Key Points of General Equilibrium:

- Multiple Markets Interaction: General equilibrium considers the interdependence of all markets (product markets and factor markets) in an economy, not just individual markets in isolation.
- Equilibrium in All Markets: Each market reaches equilibrium where the quantity supplied equals the quantity demanded. Prices adjust across markets to bring about this balance.
- Pareto Efficiency: In general equilibrium, resources are allocated in such a way that no one can be made better off without making someone else worse off, a condition known as Pareto efficiency.

Example:

- If the labor market reaches equilibrium (with a certain wage rate) and the goods market also reaches equilibrium (with a price for the product), a general equilibrium exists when all markets in the economy balance together.

Competitive markets are typically characterized by many buyers and sellers, homogenous products, and free entry and exit. In such markets, resources are allocated efficiently, ensuring that both allocative and productive efficiency are achieved.

Allocative Efficiency:

- Definition: Allocative efficiency occurs when the resources in an economy are distributed in a way that maximizes total societal welfare. This happens when goods and services are produced at the quantity where the price equals the marginal cost ($P = MC$).
- In a competitive market, firms produce goods at a price equal to the cost of producing the last unit (marginal cost). Consumers are willing

to pay a price equal to the marginal benefit they receive, so the allocation of resources results in an optimal mix of products.

Productive Efficiency:

- Definition: Productive efficiency is achieved when firms produce goods at the lowest cost, using the fewest resources necessary. In competitive markets, firms cannot sustain prices above the equilibrium level because of competition, and thus, they are forced to minimize costs and improve productivity.

Key Characteristics of Efficiency in Competitive Markets:

- Price Takers: Firms are price takers in a competitive market, meaning they must accept the market price for their products. They cannot influence the price by their own production decisions.

- No Deadweight Loss: In a perfect competitive market, there is no deadweight loss (inefficiency), which means that total surplus (consumer + producer surplus) is maximized.

- Perfect Information: Consumers and producers have perfect information about prices, products, and production methods, which ensures that market participants can make informed decisions, leading to efficient outcomes.

MODULE IX

PERFORMANCE OF AN ECONOMY – MACROERGONOMICS

Macro-economic aggregates – circular flow of macroeconomic activity – National income determination – Aggregate demand and supply – Macroeconomic equilibrium – Components of aggregate demand and national income – multiplier effect – Demand side management – Fiscal policy in theory.

Macroeconomic aggregates are broad measures that represent the overall economic performance and activity of a nation. These aggregates help economists analyze the health of an economy, identify trends, and develop policies to influence economic outcomes. The primary macroeconomic aggregates include **Gross Domestic Product (GDP)**, **unemployment rate**, **inflation rate**, **national income**, and others. These indicators provide a comprehensive view of the economic condition of a country.

1. Gross Domestic Product (GDP)
   - Definition: GDP is the total monetary value of all goods and services produced within a country's borders during a specific period (usually annually or quarterly).
   - Types of GDP:
     - Nominal GDP: Measures the value of goods and services at current market prices, without adjusting for inflation.

- Real GDP: Adjusted for inflation, showing the value of goods and services produced in constant prices.

- GDP per capita: Divides the GDP by the total population, offering an average economic output per person.

• Importance: GDP is the primary indicator of the size and health of an economy. Growth in GDP reflects economic expansion, while a decline indicates contraction.

2. **National Income**

    • Definition: National income is the total income earned by a country's residents from both domestic and foreign activities. It includes wages, profits, rents, and interest.

    • Components:

        - Wages and Salaries: Income earned by workers.

        - Profits: Income earned by businesses from their operations.

        - Rent: Income earned from land and property ownership.

        - Interest: Income from investments and loans.

    • Measurement: National income can be measured in three ways:

        - Income method: Summing up all incomes earned by factors of production.

        - Expenditure method: Summing all expenditures on final goods and services.

- Output method: Summing the value-added at each stage of production.

3. **Unemployment Rate**

    - Definition: The unemployment rate is the percentage of the labor force that is unemployed and actively seeking work.

    - Types of Unemployment:

        - Frictional Unemployment: Short-term unemployment as workers transition between jobs.

        - Structural Unemployment: Caused by changes in the structure of the economy, like technological advancements or shifts in industries.

        - Cyclical Unemployment: Occurs due to economic downturns when demand for labor decreases.

    - Importance: High unemployment signals economic distress, while low unemployment often indicates a healthy, thriving economy.

4. **Inflation Rate**

    - Definition: Inflation is the rate at which the general level of prices for goods and services is rising, and, consequently, the purchasing power of currency is falling.

    - Measurement: Inflation is measured by indices such as the Consumer Price Index (CPI) or Producer Price Index (PPI).

        - CPI measures the price change of a basket of goods and services typically consumed by households.

- PPI tracks changes in the prices received by producers for their goods and services.

- Importance: Moderate inflation is normal in a growing economy, but excessive inflation can erode purchasing power, while deflation (negative inflation) can lead to decreased economic activity and stagnation.

5. **Interest Rates**

    - Definition: Interest rates are the cost of borrowing money or the return on savings or investments, typically expressed as a percentage.

    - Role in the Economy: Central banks adjust interest rates to control economic activity. Lower interest rates stimulate borrowing and spending, while higher interest rates tend to reduce borrowing and slow down inflation.

    - Monetary Policy: Central banks, like the Federal Reserve or European Central Bank, use interest rates as a tool to regulate economic activity and stabilize prices.

6. **Balance of Payments (BOP)**

    - Definition: The balance of payments is a record of all economic transactions between residents of a country and the rest of the world.

    - Components:

        - Current Account: Includes trade in goods and services, income from investments, and transfers.

- Capital Account: Covers financial transactions such as foreign direct investment (FDI), foreign portfolio investments, and loans.

- Financial Account: Reflects changes in ownership of national assets.

• Importance: A positive BOP indicates a surplus in the economy's transactions with the rest of the world, while a deficit may point to external debt accumulation or economic imbalances.

CIRCULAR FLOW OF MACROECONOMIC ACTIVITY

The circular flow of macroeconomic activity is a fundamental concept that explains how money, goods, and services move through an economy. It illustrates the continuous exchange between different sectors (households, firms, government, and foreign sector) and how they interact to facilitate economic activity. The circular flow model helps to understand the flow of income and expenditure within an economy.

Key Sectors in the Circular Flow

1. **Households:**
    - Households represent individuals or families who provide factors of production (labor, land, capital) to firms in exchange for income (wages, rent, interest, profits).
    - Households use their income to purchase goods and services from firms in the product market.

2. **Firms (Businesses):**
   - Firms produce goods and services that are sold in the product market. They hire factors of production (labor, capital, etc.) from households.
   - Firms pay households for the use of these factors in the form of wages, rent, interest, and profits, which become the income for the household sector.

3. **Government:**
   - The government collects taxes from households and firms to finance public goods and services, such as infrastructure, education, and healthcare.
   - The government spends on public goods and transfers income (such as subsidies, unemployment benefits) to households and firms.

4. **Foreign Sector (Exports and Imports):**
   - The foreign sector refers to trade with other countries. It includes exports (goods and services sold abroad) and imports (goods and services bought from abroad).
   - The income earned from exports enters the domestic economy, while the expenditure on imports leads to an outflow of money to other countries.

The Flow of Income and Expenditure

1. **Factor Market (Resource Market):**
   - Households supply labor and other resources (land, capital) to firms. Firms, in return, pay wages, rent, and profits for the use

of these resources. This payment flows from firms to households.

2. **Product Market (Goods and Services Market):**

    - Households spend their income on goods and services produced by firms in the product market. This expenditure flows from households to firms, allowing firms to generate revenue.

3. **Government's Role:**

    - The government collects taxes from both households and firms. The revenue from taxes is used to finance public services, infrastructure, and welfare programs. Government spending flows back to households and firms in the form of public services, transfers, and subsidies.

4. **Foreign Sector:**

    - Households and firms also participate in international trade by buying and selling goods and services to and from foreign markets. Exports provide an inflow of income to the domestic economy, while imports result in an outflow of income.

The Circular Flow Model

The circular flow model can be illustrated as follows:

1. Households supply factors of production to firms in the factor market.
2. In return, firms pay wages, rent, interest, and profits to households.
3. Households use their income to purchase goods and services from firms in the product market.

4. The expenditure on goods and services flows back to firms as revenue.
5. The government collects taxes from both households and firms and redistributes them in the form of government spending.
6. The foreign sector engages with the domestic economy through exports and imports, influencing the overall flow of income.

In a more complex model, leakages and injections also play a role:

- Leakages: These are withdrawals from the circular flow of income, such as savings (when households save part of their income instead of spending it) and taxes (paid to the government). Imports also represent a leakage as money flows out of the domestic economy.
- Injections: These are additions to the circular flow, such as government spending, investments by firms, and exports. Injections increase the overall level of income and expenditure in the economy.

NATIONAL INCOME DETERMINATION

National income determination refers to the process by which the total income of a country is determined through the interaction of aggregate demand and aggregate supply in the economy. It involves analyzing the factors that influence the overall economic output and the distribution of income across various sectors.

Key Components of National Income Determination

1. **Aggregate Demand (AD):**
    - Aggregate demand is the total demand for goods and services in the economy at a given overall price level and in a given period.

It is the sum of consumption (C), investment (I), government spending (G), and net exports (NX), which is the difference between exports and imports.

- Formula: AD=C+I+G+(X−M)
- An increase in aggregate demand leads to higher national income, as firms respond by increasing production.

2. **Aggregate Supply (AS):**

    - Aggregate supply represents the total output of goods and services that firms in the economy are willing and able to produce at different price levels. In the short run, it is influenced by factors like labor, capital, and technological advancements.
    - In the long run, aggregate supply is vertical, indicating that national income is determined by factors such as resources and technology rather than the price level.

Equilibrium National Income

- National income is determined at the point where aggregate demand equals aggregate supply (i.e., where the AD curve intersects the AS curve).
- At this equilibrium level of output, the quantity of goods and services demanded equals the quantity produced, ensuring that there is no excess demand or supply in the economy.

Factors Affecting National Income

1. Consumption: The level of consumer spending is influenced by factors like income, interest rates, and consumer confidence.
2. Investment: Investments by firms depend on interest rates, business expectations, and government policies.

3. Government Spending: Fiscal policies, such as increased government spending, can directly raise national income.
4. Exports and Imports: Changes in international trade (exports and imports) can affect national income through net exports.

Aggregate demand (AD) and **aggregate supply (AS)** are essential concepts in macroErgonomics that represent the total demand and total supply in an economy, respectively. These concepts are used to understand the overall economic activity and to analyze factors like output, price levels, and national income.

AGGREGATE DEMAND (AD)

Definition: Aggregate demand is the total demand for goods and services in an economy at different price levels over a specific period. It shows the relationship between the total quantity of goods and services demanded and the overall price level in the economy.

Components of Aggregate Demand:

- Consumption (C): Spending by households on goods and services.
- Investment (I): Spending by firms on capital goods, such as machinery and buildings, and spending by households on new homes.
- Government Spending (G): Expenditures by the government on goods and services, such as defense, education, and infrastructure.
- Net Exports (NX): The difference between exports (X) and imports (M). Net exports reflect the international demand for a country's goods and services. Formula: $AD = C + I + G + (X - M)$

Factors Affecting AD:

- Interest rates: Higher interest rates reduce investment and consumption, shifting AD to the left.
- Consumer and business confidence: High confidence boosts consumption and investment, increasing AD.
- Government fiscal policy: Increased government spending or tax cuts can increase AD.

AGGREGATE SUPPLY (AS)

Definition: Aggregate supply represents the total quantity of goods and services that producers in an economy are willing to supply at different price levels over a certain period. It reflects the total output of the economy.

Short-Run Aggregate Supply (SRAS):

- In the short run, the AS curve is upward sloping, meaning that as the price level rises, producers are willing to increase output because higher prices can lead to higher profits.
- Short-run aggregate supply is influenced by factors like wages, production costs, and resource availability. If wages and input prices remain sticky in the short run, producers may increase output to meet higher demand at higher prices.

Long-Run Aggregate Supply (LRAS):

- In the long run, the aggregate supply curve is vertical, indicating that the economy's potential output (or full employment output) is determined by factors like technology, capital, and labor, not by price levels. The long-run aggregate supply reflects the economy's productive capacity.

Factors Affecting AS:

- Input prices: An increase in the price of labor, raw materials, or energy can shift the AS curve to the left.
- Technology: Technological advancements increase productivity, shifting the AS curve to the right.
- Supply shocks: Events like natural disasters or geopolitical conflicts can reduce production capacity, shifting the AS curve to the left.

MACROECONOMIC EQUILIBRIUM

Macroeconomic equilibrium occurs when the total quantity of goods and services demanded (aggregate demand) equals the total quantity of goods and services supplied (aggregate supply) in an economy at a particular price level. At this point, there is no tendency for the economy to change, meaning the output produced matches the demand for goods and services.

Key Elements of Macroeconomic Equilibrium

1. Aggregate Demand (AD): The total demand for goods and services in an economy at various price levels. It includes consumption, investment, government spending, and net exports.
2. Aggregate Supply (AS): The total supply of goods and services that producers are willing and able to supply in the economy at various price levels. It consists of both short-run and long-run aggregate supply.
3. Equilibrium Condition: The economy is in equilibrium when the aggregate demand (AD) curve intersects the aggregate supply (AS) curve. At this point, the total demand equals total supply, and there is no excess demand or supply.

Shifts in Equilibrium

- Shift in Aggregate Demand: A shift in the AD curve can cause changes in the equilibrium output and price level. For example, an increase in consumer spending can shift AD rightward, leading to higher output and prices in the short run.
- Shift in Aggregate Supply: Changes in the cost of production, like technological improvements or resource price changes, can shift the AS curve, affecting equilibrium output and price level.

COMPONENTS OF NATIONAL INCOME

National income is the total income earned by a country's residents, including all forms of income from domestic and foreign sources. It represents the overall economic activity within a nation over a specified period, typically a year. National income is calculated by summing the incomes from various sectors in the economy. The key components of national income include:

1. **Compensation of Employees**
   - This is the total income earned by workers, including wages, salaries, bonuses, and other benefits like pensions and healthcare.
   - It includes both direct wages for labor and indirect benefits from employment.
2. **Profits**
   - The income earned by businesses from their operations. Profits are the residual income that remains after deducting all business costs, such as wages, rents, and raw materials.
   - Corporate profits, as well as profits from self-employed individuals, are included.

3. **Rent**
   - Income earned from the ownership of land and property. This includes both the income derived from renting land, buildings, and natural resources.
   - Rent is considered income for the property owner, regardless of whether the property is being actively used or not.

4. **Interest**
   - Interest is income earned from lending money or from ownership of financial assets like bonds or savings accounts.
   - It represents the return on capital invested, and can include interest payments made by individuals, businesses, and government entities.

5. **Taxes and Subsidies**
   - Taxes collected by the government from households and firms, such as income tax, sales tax, and property tax, are part of national income accounting.
   - Subsidies provided by the government (such as subsidies for agriculture or energy) are subtracted to avoid overstating national income.

6. **Mixed Income**
   - Mixed income refers to the income earned by self-employed individuals, which includes both compensation for their labor and returns from their capital investment. This is typically relevant in small businesses or informal sectors.

7. **Net Exports (Exports minus Imports)**
   - The difference between a country's total exports and imports (exports − imports). Positive net exports (a trade surplus)

contribute to national income, while negative net exports (a trade deficit) reduce it.

- Exports add to national income as they represent goods and services produced domestically and consumed abroad.

The **multiplier effect** refers to the concept in Ergonomics where an initial change in spending (such as an increase in government expenditure or investment) leads to a larger overall change in national income or output. This occurs because one person's spending becomes another person's income, which in turn leads to further spending and increases in demand throughout the economy.

How the Multiplier Effect Works:

1. Initial Injection: An initial increase in spending, such as government expenditure, investment by businesses, or exports, leads to an increase in the income of those who receive the spending (e.g., workers, suppliers).
2. Increased Consumption: The recipients of the initial spending then use their additional income to consume more goods and services. This increases the demand for goods and services in the economy.
3. Further Spending: As demand rises, firms respond by increasing production, leading to more income for workers and suppliers. These workers and suppliers then spend part of their additional income, generating a further increase in demand.
4. Repeated Cycle: The process repeats itself multiple times, with each round of spending leading to an increase in national income. The total change in income is larger than the initial change in spending due to the repeated rounds of consumption.
5. The size of the multiplier depends on the marginal propensity to consume (MPC), which is the proportion of additional income that

consumers spend. The formula for the multiplier is: Multiplier = $1/(1-MPC)$

Where:

- MPC is the marginal propensity to consume (the fraction of additional income that is spent on consumption).

DEMAND-SIDE MANAGEMENT (DSM)

Demand-Side Management (DSM) refers to strategies and programs aimed at influencing consumer demand for goods and services, especially in energy and utility sectors, to achieve economic, environmental, or operational objectives. The goal of DSM is to optimize and control demand, ensuring that consumption aligns with available resources, infrastructure, and cost considerations.

Key Objectives of Demand-Side Management:

1. Reduce Peak Demand: DSM aims to smooth out peaks in demand (e.g., electricity usage) to prevent overloading of systems and reduce the need for additional infrastructure investments.
2. Energy Conservation: Encourage consumers to reduce their overall energy consumption, leading to reduced environmental impact, lower costs, and efficient resource use.
3. Cost Management: By controlling demand and promoting energy efficiency, DSM helps to manage costs for both consumers and utilities, making energy consumption more affordable.
4. Sustainable Development: By reducing excess demand and promoting efficiency, DSM supports environmental sustainability by reducing the need for additional energy production, which may come from non-renewable sources.

Benefits of Demand-Side Management:

- Improved Grid Stability: Reducing peak demand lessens the pressure on energy supply systems, preventing blackouts and reducing the need for additional power plants.
- Cost Savings: By managing consumption, consumers can lower their energy bills, and utilities can avoid costly infrastructure upgrades.
- Environmental Impact: Reduced energy demand leads to a lower carbon footprint, contributing to environmental sustainability.
- Efficient Resource Use: DSM ensures that resources are used more efficiently, reducing waste and optimizing available supply.

FISCAL POLICY IN THEORY

Fiscal policy refers to the use of government spending and taxation policies to influence the overall economic activity, stabilize the economy, and achieve macroeconomic objectives such as full employment, price stability, and economic growth. Fiscal policy is a key tool in the hands of the government to manage the economy and address issues like inflation, unemployment, and recessions.

Objectives of Fiscal Policy:

- Economic Growth: Stimulating growth by increasing government spending or cutting taxes to boost demand in the economy.
- Price Stability: Managing inflation through reducing government expenditure or increasing taxes to curb demand.

- Full Employment: Reducing unemployment by boosting aggregate demand through fiscal interventions like public works or subsidies.
- Income Distribution: Reducing income inequality by using progressive taxation systems or welfare programs.
- Balance of Payments: Addressing trade imbalances and ensuring sustainable foreign exchange reserves

Types of Fiscal Policy:

1. **Expansionary Fiscal Policy:**

    - Used during economic downturns or recessions.
    - Involves increasing government spending, cutting taxes, or both, to boost aggregate demand.
    - Designed to stimulate economic activity, reduce unemployment, and increase production.

2. **Contractionary Fiscal Policy:**

    - Used when the economy is overheating or during periods of high inflation.
    - Involves reducing government spending and/or increasing taxes to decrease aggregate demand.
    - Aims to cool down the economy and control inflation.

Fiscal Policy Tools:

1. **Government Expenditure**
   - Direct spending on projects like infrastructure, healthcare, education, and defense to create jobs and increase demand in the economy.

2. **Tax Policy:**
   - Changing the tax rates (e.g., income tax, corporate tax) to influence the amount of disposable income in the hands of households and firms.

3. **Public Borrowing:**
   - The government may borrow funds (through the issuance of bonds) to finance its expenditures, especially when there's a budget deficit.

Limitations of Fiscal Policy:

1. **Time Lags:**
   - Fiscal policy actions can take time to be implemented due to delays in decision making, legislative processes, and the execution of government spending projects.

2. **Crowding Out:**
   - Increased government borrowing to finance fiscal policy can lead to higher interest rates, which may reduce private investment (crowding out).

3. **Political Constraints:**
    - Fiscal policy decisions may be influenced by political considerations, leading to suboptimal policy choices that may not align with economic needs.

4. **Inflationary Pressures:**
    - If expansionary fiscal policies are used excessively, they can lead to higher inflation, particularly in an economy that is near full employment.

MODULE X

AGGREGATE SUPPLY AND THE ROLE OF MONEY

Short-run and Long-run supply curve – Unemployment and its impact – Okun's law – Inflation and the impact – reasons for inflation – Demand Vs Supply factors –Inflation Vs Unemployement tradeoff – Phillips curve – short- run and long-run –Supply side Policy and management- Money market- Demand and supply of money – money-market equilibrium and national income – the role of monetary policy.

Short-Run Supply Curve

The short-run individual supply curve is the individual's marginal cost at all points greater than the minimum average variable cost. It holds true because a firm will not produce if the market price is less than the shut-down price.

Ultimately, the short-run individual supply curve demonstrates how the producer's profit maximizing output is strictly dependent on the market price and holds the fixed cost as sunk.

Short Run Supply Curve of a Competitive Firm

The supply curve of a perfectly competitive firm has a unique characteristic: it appears as a horizontal line at the market price. This feature stems from the core principles of perfect competition, where firms are price-takers, accepting the prevailing market price and adjusting their output accordingly. In this market structure, each firm's marginal cost curve functions as its short run supply curve, representing the quantity of output the firm is willing to supply at different price levels.

As long as the market price exceeds the firm's average variable cost, it will continue to produce in the short run, even if it incurs losses. However, if the market price drops below the average variable cost, the firm will halt production in the short run. Therefore, a perfectly competitive firm's horizontal short run supply curve demonstrates its ability to respond to market conditions, with output levels adjusting to match the marginal cost with the current market price.

The firm produces where the market price (P) equals the marginal cost (MC): P = MC.

If P ≥ AVC, the firm supplies output to the market.

If P < AVC, the firm halts production to minimise losses.

Short Run Supply Curve of a Perfectly Competitive Firm

The supply curve of a perfectly competitive firm is uniquely characterised by a horizontal line at the market price. This results from the nature of perfect competition, where firms are price-takers and must accept the prevailing market price, adjusting their output accordingly. In this context, each firm's marginal cost curve acts as its short run supply curve, reflecting the quantity of output the firm is willing to supply at different price levels. As long as the market price is at or above the firm's average variable cost, the firm will continue to produce, even if it incurs losses.

However, if the market price falls below the average variable cost, the firm will stop production in the short run. Thus, a perfectly competitive firm's horizontal short run supply curve demonstrates its responsiveness to market conditions, with output levels adjusting to match the marginal cost to the market price.

LONG RUN SUPPLY CURVE

The long-run supply curve of a firm is a dynamic concept that unveils the intricacies of production decisions, cost considerations, and industry dynamics when all factors of production can be adjusted. It showcases how firms respond to changing market conditions, technological advancements, and shifts in demand and supply. The various shapes of the long-run supply curve – perfectly elastic, perfectly inelastic, and upward-sloping – reveal the diverse characteristics of industries and their production capabilities.

Economies and diseconomies of scale, entry and exit dynamics, and the interplay between cost structures and market demand all contribute to the positioning of a firm on the long-run supply curve. This concept has far-reaching implications for market equilibrium, industry competition, and the allocation of resources across sectors.

Long-run supply curves can take different shapes based on the characteristics of the industry. The three primary shapes are perfectly elastic, perfectly inelastic, and upward-sloping.

1. A perfectly Elastic long-run Supply Curve: occurs when firms can increase their output without affecting the market price. Each firm can expand its production without impacting the overall market price in industries with homogenous and easily scalable products, such as agricultural goods.

2. Perfectly Inelastic long-run Supply Curve: In contrast to the previous scenario, this occurs when the market price remains constant regardless of the quantity supplied. This is rare and usually associated with unique goods or services where firms cannot increase their output due to limited resources or regulatory restrictions.

3. Upward-Sloping long-run Supply Curve: This is the most common shape for long-run supply curves. It signifies that as production increases, the market price also increases. This occurs when industries have finite resources, and as firms expand production, costs rise due to diminishing returns to scale or scarcity of inputs.

Unemployment refers to the condition where individuals who are capable of working, are actively seeking work but are unable to find employment. It is a major economic issue that has far-reaching consequences not only for individuals but for society and the economy as a whole.

Impact of Unemployment:

1. **Economic Growth and Output:**

    - Unemployment reduces the overall productive capacity of an economy. When people are out of work, the economy operates below its potential output, leading to lower GDP and slower economic growth.

2. **Increased Government Spending:**

    - High unemployment leads to increased government expenditure on welfare benefits, unemployment insurance, and social security programs, straining public finances.

3. **Inflationary Pressures:**

    - While unemployment often reduces inflationary pressures (as demand for goods and services decreases), prolonged high unemployment can lead to wage deflation, as workers may accept lower wages due to a lack of job opportunities.

4. **Social Consequences:**
   - Unemployment can lead to social instability, as individuals face increased stress, social exclusion, and reduced quality of life. Long-term unemployment can contribute to issues like poverty, family breakdown, and increased crime rates.

5. **Loss of Human Capital:**
   - Prolonged unemployment can lead to skill degradation as individuals are not able to keep up with the demands of the job market. This makes it harder for the unemployed to find work, even when economic conditions improve.

6. **Psychological Impact:**
   - Unemployment can lead to mental health issues, including stress, depression, and anxiety, due to financial strain and the loss of social identity tied to employment.

7. **Reduced Consumer Spending:**
   - Unemployed individuals have less disposable income, which reduces their ability to spend on goods and services, thereby reducing overall demand in the economy and exacerbating the effects of a recession.

8. **Inequality:**
   - Unemployment often disproportionately affects certain segments of the population, particularly marginalized groups such as younger workers, minorities, and those with lower educational levels, leading to greater income inequality.

OKUN'S LAW

Okun's Law is an empirical relationship between unemployment and economic output, formulated by economist Arthur Okun in the early 1960s. The law suggests that for every 1% increase in the unemployment rate above the natural rate of unemployment, a country's Gross Domestic Product (GDP) will be roughly an additional 2% lower than its potential output. In simple terms, it connects changes in unemployment to changes in real GDP.

Key Concepts of Okun's Law:

1. Natural Rate of Unemployment: This is the level of unemployment that exists when the economy is at full employment, which includes frictional and structural unemployment but excludes cyclical unemployment. When the actual unemployment rate exceeds this level, it implies that the economy is underperforming.

2. GDP and Unemployment Relationship: Okun's Law implies a negative relationship between the unemployment rate and GDP growth. Higher unemployment leads to a lower level of economic output. This is because unemployed people are not contributing to production, thus reducing the economy's total output.

3. Okun's Coefficient: The law is often expressed as a formula:

$$\Delta Y = -k \times \Delta U$$

Where:
- ΔY = Change in GDP
- ΔU = Change in unemployment rate
- k is the constant (usually around 2 in most countries).

For example, if the unemployment rate increases by 1%, GDP could decrease by approximately 2% as per Okun's Law.

Inflation refers to the persistent increase in the general price level of goods and services in an economy over time. While moderate inflation can indicate a growing economy, excessive inflation can lead to a range of negative economic and social impacts.

Impacts of Inflation:

1. **Reduced Purchasing Power**
   - Inflation erodes the value of money, meaning that consumers can buy less with the same amount of money. This impacts individuals, especially those on fixed incomes, as their purchasing power declines.

2. **Income Inequality:**
   - Inflation tends to disproportionately affect low-income groups because they spend a larger portion of their income on essential goods and services that become more expensive. Wealthier individuals, particularly those with assets, may be better able to protect themselves from inflation.

3. **Uncertainty and Economic Instability:**
   - High inflation creates uncertainty about future prices, making it difficult for businesses and consumers to make long-term financial decisions. This can slow down investment and savings, as businesses may be reluctant to invest in a volatile environment.

4. **Interest Rates and Borrowing Costs:**
   - Central banks often raise interest rates to control high inflation. Higher interest rates increase the cost of borrowing for both

consumers and businesses, reducing spending and investment. This can slow economic growth and dampen consumer demand.

5. **Distorted Price Signals:**

    - Inflation can distort the signals that prices provide about supply and demand in the economy. Price increases may reflect inflationary pressures rather than changes in real demand, leading to inefficient allocation of resources and potentially causing shortages or surpluses.

6. **Wage-Price Spiral:**

    - When inflation rises, workers often demand higher wages to keep up with the rising cost of living. In turn, businesses increase prices to cover higher wage costs, which can trigger further inflation, creating a cycle known as the wageprice spiral.

7. **Impact on Savings and Investments:**

    - Inflation reduces the real value of savings. If the inflation rate exceeds the interest rate earned on savings, the purchasing power of those savings declines. Similarly, inflation can reduce the value of fixed-income investments, such as bonds.

8. **Balance of Payments and Trade Deficits:**

    - Inflation can affect international trade by making a country's goods and services more expensive relative to those of other countries. This can reduce exports and increase imports, potentially leading to trade imbalances and a weakening of the national currency.

Reasons for Inflation

- 1. **Demand-Pull Inflation:**
    - Occurs when aggregate demand exceeds aggregate supply, leading to price increases.
    - Causes: Increased consumer spending, government spending, higher investment, and foreign demand.

- 2. **Cost-Push Inflation:**
    - Happens when production costs rise, leading firms to raise prices.
    - Causes: Higher raw material costs, rising wages, supply chain disruptions, and currency depreciation.

- 3. **Built-In Inflation (Wage-Price Spiral):**
    - Occurs when the expectation of rising prices leads to higher wages, which in turn leads to higher prices.
    - Causes: Inflation expectations, and a cycle of rising wages and prices.

- 4. **Structural Factors:**
    - Related to inefficiencies or monopolies in the economy.
    - Causes: Market power of firms, and shifts in industry structures.

- 5. **Monetary Factors:**
    - Occurs when there's an increase in the money supply.
    - Causes: Excessive money printing, and monetary policies like low-interest rates.

- 6. **External Factors:**
    - Global events or changes in commodity prices affecting domestic inflation.

- Causes: Rising global commodity prices, oil price increases, and global economic conditions.

DEMAND VS. SUPPLY FACTORS

Demand factors and supply factors both play a crucial role in determining prices and quantities in an economy. They are the key drivers of market equilibrium and influence economic outcomes such as inflation, production levels, and overall market efficiency.

Demand Factors:

These factors affect the demand side of the market, influencing how much consumers are willing to buy at different price levels.

1. Income Levels: Higher incomes increase demand for goods and services, shifting the demand curve to the right.
2. Consumer Preferences: Changes in consumer tastes and preferences can increase or decrease demand for certain products.
3. Price of Substitutes: An increase in the price of a substitute product can increase demand for the product in question.
4. Price of Complements: If the price of a complementary good decreases, demand for the associated product may rise.
5. Expectations: If consumers expect prices to rise in the future, current demand may increase as people buy in anticipation.
6. Population and Demographics: A growing population or changes in demographics can increase overall market demand.

Supply Factors:

These factors influence the supply side of the market, affecting how much producers are willing to sell at different price levels.

1. Production Costs: Higher production costs (e.g., wages, raw materials) can reduce supply, shifting the supply curve to the left.

2. Technology: Advances in technology can reduce production costs and increase supply.
3. Government Policies: Taxes, subsidies, and regulations can either encourage or discourage supply. High taxes or regulations can reduce supply, while subsidies can increase it.
4. Availability of Resources: If key resources (e.g., labor, raw materials) become scarce, supply can decrease.
5. Expectations: If producers expect higher prices in the future, they may reduce current supply to sell at higher prices later.
6. Number of Producers: An increase in the number of producers in the market can increase the overall supply.

INFLATION VS. UNEMPLOYMENT TRADE-OFF (THE PHILLIPS CURVE)

The **inflation-unemployment trade-off** refers to the inverse relationship between inflation and unemployment in the short run, often illustrated by the **Phillips Curve**. According to this concept, there is a perceived trade-off between the two: as unemployment decreases, inflation tends to rise, and vice versa. **Short-Run Phillips Curve:**

• Relationship: In the short term, the Phillips Curve suggests that lower unemployment is associated with higher inflation and higher unemployment with lower inflation. This is because when the labor market is tight (low unemployment), workers demand higher wages, leading to increased production costs for businesses. To maintain profitability, businesses raise prices, resulting in inflation.

• Graphical Representation: The curve slopes downward, reflecting the inverse relationship between inflation and unemployment. When inflation is low, unemployment is high, and vice versa.

- Example: In a growing economy with low unemployment, businesses face pressure to pay higher wages to attract workers, leading to increased production costs and, ultimately, higher prices (inflation).

Long-Run Phillips Curve:

In the long run, the relationship between inflation and unemployment becomes more complicated. According to economists like Milton Friedman and Edmund Phelps, the Phillips Curve in the long run is vertical at the natural rate of unemployment (also known as the NonAccelerating Inflation Rate of Unemployment, or NAIRU).

- Natural Rate of Unemployment: This is the level of unemployment that the economy naturally gravitates toward when inflation expectations are stable. In the long run, no trade-off exists between inflation and unemployment because the economy adjusts to a level of unemployment determined by factors like labor market dynamics and structural characteristics of the economy.
- Expectations-Adjusted Phillips Curve: Over time, as people adjust their expectations for inflation, the economy returns to the natural rate of unemployment. If inflation is persistently high, workers will demand higher wages, and businesses will continue raising prices, leading to a new higher inflation rate, but with no lasting decrease in unemployment.
  - Example: If a government tries to reduce unemployment below the natural rate by increasing demand (through expansionary policies), it might reduce unemployment temporarily, but inflation will rise. Eventually, the economy will adjust, and unemployment will return to its natural rate with higher inflation. Expectations and the Role of Credibility:

The expectations-augmented Phillips Curve suggests that inflation is influenced not only by current levels of unemployment but also by what people expect in the future. If businesses and workers expect inflation to rise, they will act in ways that drive inflation up, even if unemployment is high.

- Adaptive Expectations: In this model, people form their expectations about future inflation based on past inflation. If inflation has been high, people expect it to continue, which drives inflation even when unemployment is high.

- Rational Expectations: In this model, individuals and firms form their expectations based on all available information, including future policies. If they expect inflation to be controlled in the future (e.g., through tight monetary policy), they might not demand higher wages or raise prices, helping to break the inflation-unemployment trade-off.

The **Phillips Curve** provides a useful framework for understanding the short-run trade-off between inflation and unemployment. In the short run, low unemployment often leads to higher inflation, while high unemployment can lead to lower inflation. However, in the long run, the relationship becomes less clear, as the economy adjusts and returns to a natural rate of unemployment, with inflation expectations playing a critical role. Policymakers must consider these dynamics when trying to balance inflation and unemployment to achieve stable economic growth.

SUPPLY-SIDE POLICY AND MANAGEMENT

Supply-side policies are economic policies aimed at increasing the productive capacity of an economy by improving the supply of goods and services. Unlike demand-side policies, which focus on increasing aggregate demand, supply-side policies focus on improving the supply side of the economy, particularly through enhancing production, increasing efficiency, and promoting long-term growth. The primary goal is to boost output, reduce costs, and create a more competitive economy.

Main Supply-Side Policies:

1. **Tax Cuts:**
   - Corporate Tax Cuts: Lowering corporate taxes incentivizes businesses to invest in capital, expand production, and increase efficiency. This can lead to higher output and lower prices.
   - Income Tax Cuts: Reducing income taxes on individuals encourages people to work more, save, and invest, thereby increasing the labor supply and productivity.

2. **Deregulation:**
   - Reducing government regulations (e.g., environmental, labor laws, business operations) helps reduce the cost of doing business, increases efficiency, and encourages entrepreneurship and competition.
   - Example: Streamlining business registration processes, cutting red tape, or easing labor market regulations.

3. **Investment in Education and Training:**
   - Enhancing the quality of education and job training programs ensures that the workforce possesses the necessary skills for high-productivity jobs and technological advancements.
   - Goal: Increase human capital, improve labor productivity, and foster innovation.

4. **Labor Market Reforms:**
   - Policies aimed at reducing labor market rigidity, such as lowering minimum wages or easing hiring and firing regulations, can make the labor market more flexible.

- Example: Making it easier for businesses to hire or fire workers or offering tax incentives for businesses to hire disadvantaged groups.

5. **Infrastructure Investment:**
   - Government spending on infrastructure (e.g., roads, communication, energy, transport) reduces operational costs for businesses, enhances productivity, and improves economic efficiency.
   - Goal: Improve supply chains and create a more business-friendly environment.

6. **Promotion of Innovation and Technology:**
   - Encouraging research and development (R&D) through grants, tax credits, and government-sponsored programs fosters technological innovation, which can improve productivity. o Goal: Drive technological progress, improve production processes, and increase the efficiency of businesses.

7. **Trade Liberalization:**
   - Reducing tariffs, trade barriers, and import restrictions allows businesses to access cheaper raw materials, labor, and markets abroad, thereby improving their competitiveness and lowering costs.
   - Goal: Increase market competition, boost efficiency, and lower consumer prices.

8. **Privatization and Encouraging Competition:**
   - Privatizing state-owned enterprises and fostering competition in markets can improve efficiency, reduce costs, and lead to better services and products.
   - Goal: Increase market-driven efficiency and innovation.

9. **Encouraging Savings and Investment:**
    - Policies that encourage saving and investment, such as offering tax incentives for long-term savings or promoting investment funds, can lead to greater capital formation and productivity.
    - Goal: Increase the capital available for business expansion and innovation.

Challenges of Supply-Side Policies:
1. Initial Costs: Some supply-side policies, such as infrastructure investment or tax cuts, may lead to increased government spending in the short term, causing budget deficits.
2. Inequality: While supply-side policies can benefit the economy as a whole, they may lead to greater income inequality if the benefits are not evenly distributed.
3. Time Lag: The benefits of supply-side policies, such as improved education or infrastructure, may take years or even decades to materialize.
4. Implementation Issues: Deregulation and labor market reforms may face resistance from unions, environmental groups, and other stakeholders.

Supply-Side Management:

Effective supply-side management focuses on implementing and managing these policies in a way that maximizes their potential benefits for the economy. Key aspects include:

- Strategic Planning: Governments must carefully design policies that align with long-term economic goals and address current constraints.
- Coordination with Other Policies: Supply-side policies should work in conjunction with fiscal and monetary policies to ensure overall economic stability.

- Monitoring and Evaluation: Ongoing monitoring is necessary to evaluate the effectiveness of supply-side policies and make adjustments as needed.

MONEY MARKET

The **money market** is a sector of the financial market where short-term borrowing and lending of funds take place, typically involving instruments with maturities of less than one year. It provides a mechanism for managing short-term liquidity and ensures the stability of interest rates in the economy.

Key Features of the Money Market:

1. Short-Term: Transactions typically involve financial instruments with a maturity of one year or less.
2. High Liquidity: The instruments traded are highly liquid, meaning they can be quickly converted into cash without significant loss of value.
3. Low Risk: Money market instruments are generally considered low-risk due to their short-term nature and high credit quality.

Functions of the Money Market:

1. Liquidity Management: Helps businesses, banks, and governments manage their shortterm funding needs and ensure that they have enough cash on hand.
2. Interest Rate Determination: The money market plays a key role in influencing short-term interest rates, which can affect the overall economy.
3. Safe Investment Options: Provides low-risk investment opportunities for investors looking for safety and liquidity.

Importance of the Money Market:

- Stabilizes the Economy: Ensures smooth functioning by offering a platform for managing short-term financial needs.
- Supports Monetary Policy: Central banks use the money market to implement monetary policy, such as controlling inflation and managing interest rates.

DEMAND AND SUPPLY OF MONEY

The **demand and supply of money** is a key concept in monetary Ergonomics, influencing interest rates, inflation, and overall economic activity. The interaction between money supply (controlled by the central bank) and money demand (determined by the public) affects the economy's stability.

Demand for Money:

- Definition: The demand for money refers to the desire of households and businesses to hold liquid assets, such as cash or easily accessible bank deposits, rather than invest in other assets.
- Factors Influencing Money Demand:
    - Income Levels: Higher income leads to increased transactions, which increases the demand for money.
    - Interest Rates: Higher interest rates encourage people to hold less money in liquid form and invest in interest-bearing assets, reducing money demand.
    - Price Levels: As prices rise (inflation), more money is needed to carry out transactions.

- Economic Activity: In times of economic growth, people demand more money for consumption and investment.
- Transaction Motive: People hold money to conduct everyday transactions.
- Precautionary Motive: People demand money for unforeseen expenses.

Supply of Money:

- Definition: The supply of money is the total amount of money available in the economy, controlled by the central bank and commercial banks.
- Central Bank's Role: The central bank (e.g., the Federal Reserve in the U.S.) controls the money supply through tools such as:
    - Open Market Operations (OMOs): Buying and selling government securities to influence the money supply.
    - Discount Rate: The interest rate charged to commercial banks for borrowing from the central bank, affecting the lending capacity of banks.
    - Reserve Requirements: The amount of reserves banks must hold, affecting the amount of money they can lend out.
- Monetary Policy: By adjusting the money supply, the central bank can influence economic conditions, such as inflation and unemployment.

Money market equilibrium refers to the condition where the demand for money equals the supply of money in the economy. This equilibrium is important because it helps determine the interest rate, which in turn affects investment, consumption, and overall economic activity, including **national income**.

Money Market Equilibrium occurs when the demand for money equals the supply of money. At this point, interest rates stabilize, and the economy functions efficiently.

- If Money Supply > Money Demand: There is excess money in the economy, which can lead to inflationary pressures.
- If Money Supply < Money Demand: A shortage of money can drive up interest rates and potentially reduce economic activity.

The equilibrium in the money market is crucial for determining national income and economic activity. Here's how they are related:

1. Interest Rates and Investment:

    • Interest Rates play a key role in influencing investment decisions. When interest rates are low (often due to an excess supply of money), borrowing becomes cheaper, encouraging businesses to invest in new projects, expansion, or capital goods. This increases aggregate demand and, ultimately, national income.

    • Higher Interest Rates (due to excess demand for money) make borrowing more expensive, potentially reducing investment and slowing economic growth.

2. Liquidity Preference and Consumption:

    • As national income rises, people engage in more transactions, leading to higher demand for money. To meet this demand, the central bank may increase the money supply, which can lower interest rates, making borrowing cheaper and stimulating investment and consumption.

- If the supply of money does not adjust to rising demand (due to an increase in national income), interest rates might rise, discouraging investment and reducing economic activity.

3. Monetary Policy Impact:

    - Central banks manage money supply to influence national income. For instance, in times of recession, the central bank might increase the money supply to lower interest rates and stimulate investment and consumption, boosting national income.

    - Conversely, to control inflation, the central bank might reduce the money supply, increasing interest rates, reducing investment, and slowing down economic activity.

4. Aggregate Demand and National Income:

    - The money market equilibrium affects aggregate demand through its impact on interest rates. Lower interest rates can increase aggregate demand by encouraging investment and consumer spending. Conversely, higher interest rates can reduce aggregate demand and slow down economic growth.

    - As national income grows, so does the demand for money (due to higher transactions), and the central bank may adjust the money supply to maintain equilibrium. This interplay between national income and the money market is critical for maintaining economic stability.

ROLE OF MONETARY POLICY

Monetary policy refers to the actions taken by a country's central bank (such as the Federal Reserve, European Central Bank, or Reserve Bank of India) to manage the money supply, control inflation, stabilize the currency, and achieve sustainable economic growth. It is a crucial tool for managing the economy, influencing key variables like interest rates, inflation, employment, and overall economic activity.

Key Objectives of Monetary Policy:

1. Price Stability (Control Inflation)

    - One of the primary goals of monetary policy is to control inflation. By adjusting interest rates and managing the money supply, central banks can influence the inflation rate, ensuring that it stays within a target range (often 2% in many economies).

    - Higher interest rates typically reduce consumer spending and business investment, helping to curb inflation.

    - Lower interest rates stimulate spending and investment, potentially increasing inflation if the economy is overheating.

2. **Economic Growth:**

    - Central banks use monetary policy to promote economic growth by influencing the cost and availability of credit. When interest rates are low, businesses and consumers are more likely to borrow and spend, which stimulates economic activity.

- By adjusting the money supply, central banks can ensure that there is sufficient liquidity to support economic growth without triggering inflation.

3. **Employment:**

    - Monetary policy can help reduce unemployment by stimulating economic activity. Lower interest rates encourage investment and consumption, leading to higher demand for goods and services, and thus more job creation.

    - The central bank can act counter-cyclically by easing monetary policy during recessions (lowering interest rates and increasing money supply) to stimulate demand and job creation.

4. **Stabilizing the Currency:**

    - Central banks also use monetary policy to influence exchange rates and ensure that the national currency remains stable. A stable currency is important for international trade and investor confidence.

    - Changes in interest rates can impact the attractiveness of a country's currency. Higher interest rates can attract foreign investment, strengthening the currency, while lower rates may lead to depreciation.

Impact of Monetary Policy on the Economy:

1. Inflation Control: By managing the money supply and interest rates, central banks can control inflation, which helps preserve the purchasing power of the currency.

2. Economic Growth: Well-managed monetary policy can encourage sustainable growth by stimulating demand during economic downturns or cooling down an overheating economy.

3. Employment: Lower interest rates generally encourage business investment, which can lead to job creation. Conversely, higher rates can reduce demand and slow down hiring.

4. Consumer Confidence: A predictable and stable monetary policy boosts consumer confidence, as people feel assured that inflation will remain stable and that interest rates will not be excessively high.

www.ingramcontent.com/pod-product-compliance
Lightning Source LLC
Chambersburg PA
CBHW021148160426
43194CB00007B/742